Praise for
THE LEADERSHIP ANTHEM

The Leadership Anthem is a call-and-response from music to leadership. This intensely valuable leadership framework offers unique and compelling concepts to move your leadership practice to the next level.

DR. NANCY TENANT, innovation expert, leadership author, and professor at University of Chicago Booth School of Business

I appreciate *The Leadership Anthem*'s Ensemble Model for its ability to clearly demonstrate that all roles are critical and each one of us is a leader serving in different capacities. As an executive, this allows me to lean into people's strengths and contributions. It stands in opposition to strict hierarchical leadership models that have leaders only at the top, forcing key players into roles that often don't allow them to lead at their best.

CHRIS SCHYVINCK, CEO and chairperson, Shure Incorporated

The Leadership Anthem taps into a unique musical method for learning the foundational skills of leadership. This book emphasizes the skills leaders need to succeed in this new era of work.

DON VANPOOL, leadership coach, former GE executive leader, and former infantry officer, 82nd Airborne Division, US Army

It's no accident that a musical collaboration is often called a "work." There are endless parallels between music and leadership that *The Leadership Anthem* uniquely and compellingly explores. Using clear and practical case histories, Kohler repeatedly left me nodding my head as he made meaningful and impactful connections between musical ensembles and corporate team dynamics. As a lifelong musician and corporate leader myself, I recognize Kohler's deep experience in creating this compelling score.
AMEET MALLIK, president and CEO, ADC Therapeutics

Stephen Kohler has a singular sensibility matched with an openness and inquisitive curiosity. It is this same sensibility that is the bedrock of *The Leadership Anthem*—an approach that Kohler challenges us to adopt to gain a fresh perspective on leadership that, while initially counterintuitive, ultimately makes perfect sense. As a producer, I reveled in the book's extended musical metaphors and found myself gaining new insights into music alongside the book's profound leadership lessons. Among musicians, roles are often seen as horizontally interconnected, with no one role overshadowing another. Kohler's Ensemble Model translates this harmonious dynamic into the workplace, providing a blueprint for collaborative leadership. Whether you see yourself as a Composer, Conductor, Performer, Producer, or Fan, you will find inspiration, encouragement, and motivation within the pages of *The Leadership Anthem*.
LIAM DAVIS, five-time Grammy®-nominated producer

Leading with values and vibes is everything. Stephen Kohler has tapped into this truth and uses music as an accessible way to explore and develop these critical motivators.
MATT McCONNELL, founder and co-CEO, Intradiem

In *The Leadership Anthem*, Stephen Kohler has masterfully woven his love of music with his passion for executive coaching. What's emerged is a groundbreaking approach to leadership development that hits every note!

CHRIS STEPHEN, executive leader, formerly of Weber-Stephen Products

As a physician, I have dedicated my life to helping people to be able to hear physically, but hearing is not the same as listening. The best leaders must listen to diverse perspectives. They use their eyes, ears, and brain to understand what's being said beyond what's explicitly stated. *The Leadership Anthem* rightly defines listening as the core of leadership.

CHAD RUFFIN, MD, cochlear implant surgeon and ENT

It's about time Stephen Kohler put his leadership model into a book! Our organization is a frequent flier for his music-based keynotes and workshops that bring leaders out of their day-to-days to contemplate their leadership in a new context that is relatable, engaging, and inspiring.

BOB CAPPADONA, president and CEO, Veolia North America

THE
LEADERSHIP
ANTHEM

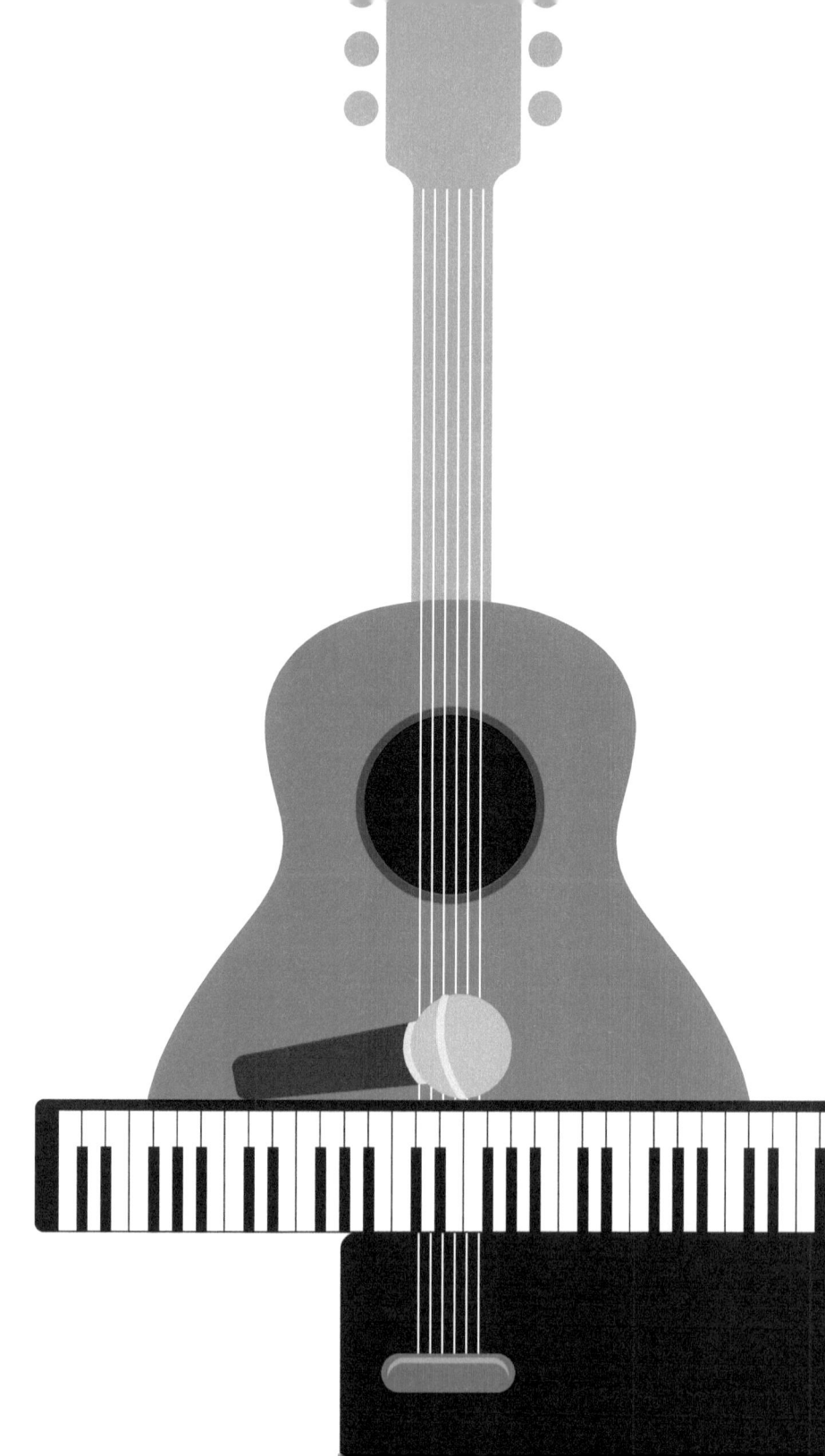

THE LEADERSHIP ANTHEM

How Listening like a Musician Creates Strong Performances

STEPHEN J. KOHLER

● ● **PAGE TWO**

Copyright © 2025 by Stephen J. Kohler

All rights reserved. No part of this book may be reproduced, stored in a retrieval system or transmitted, in any form or by any means, without the prior written consent of the publisher, except in the case of brief quotations, embodied in reviews and articles.

Original lyrics to Audira song used by permission
© Stephen Kohler Music

Some names and identifying details have been changed or withheld to protect the privacy of individuals.

Cataloguing in publication information is available from Library and Archives Canada.

ISBN 978-1-77458-538-2 (paperback)
ISBN 978-1-77458-537-5 (ebook)

Page Two
pagetwo.com

Edited by Sarah Brohman
Copyedited by Rachel Ironstone
Cover design by Jennifer Lum
Interior design by Cameron McKague
Interior illustrations by Jeff Winocur

audiralabs.com | stephenjkohler.com

For Mom, the best writer and reading buddy I ever knew

CONTENTS

FOREWORD by Harry L. Davis *1*

Overture *3*

1 **FEEL THE MUSIC:**
Find Your Heart as a Leader *15*

2 **EAR TRAINING:**
Listen like a Musician *27*

3 **THE AUDIRA ENSEMBLE MODEL:**
The Five Leadership Roles *49*

4 **THE COMPOSER:**
Establish Values, Mission, and Vision *57*

5 **THE CONDUCTOR:**
Create Space for Others to Succeed *69*

6 **THE PERFORMER:**
Maximize Your Dynamic Range *87*

7 **THE PRODUCER:**
Bring Out the Best in Others *103*

8 **THE FAN:**
Follow, Celebrate, Support *113*

9 **THE TOUR:**
Listen Closely, and Improvise like a Jazz Pro *123*

Coda *131*

Acknowledgments *137*

Notes *141*

Sources and Resources *147*

FOREWORD

YOU WILL find an abundance of material in this book that is relevant to your life and leadership.

Leadership rests on having knowledge and tools that *generalize* across different situations but also *individualize* through the display of one's unique talents. Leadership is also fundamentally performative, which is why the performing arts serve as such a valuable resource in honing leadership skills. The worlds of arts and leadership are often seen as different from and even foreign to each other. Yet the arts are actually a rich source of insights and tools that can be utilized every day in both your professional and personal lives.

My leadership work has involved bringing concepts from theater into my teaching of MBA students and executives. The classroom is where I had the great pleasure of meeting Stephen and learned that his passion closely aligned with mine. Stephen, following a long and successful career in business, has made a commitment to utilizing musical concepts to help strengthen leaders' performances (in a corporate sense as well as a musical one). When I asked if he would consider participating in our leadership course at the University of Chicago, he enthusiastically said yes and has over the past five years contributed in meaningful ways.

Music is a powerful force in almost every part of life. It is seen as an expression of will and emotion, and it brings people together through deep listening. It involves practice and learning from mistakes. There can be harmony—but also dissonance at times, which can open the listener to new ways of experiencing the world. Beyond the notes played in a performance, tempo and volume can help someone to feel joyous or sad and to experience both the known and unknown. Music works well as a metaphor for leadership since many of the qualities found in music—including harmony, dissonance, tempo, and volume—can be found within an organization and as part of a manager's job.

Stephen Kohler grounds these qualities in five interrelated roles of the leader: Composer, Conductor, Performer, Producer, and Fan. Further, he connects each of these roles to specific examples drawn from his rich experiences in working with a variety of leaders.

This book is well worth exploring and its musical lessons worth incorporating into your performances. It may bring the many audiences in your life to sustained applause and even to shout "Encore!" That's because they themselves will flourish and grow as a result of your reading this.

Harry L. Davis

Roger L. and Rachel M. Goetz Distinguished Service Professor Emeritus of Creative Management
University of Chicago Booth School of Business

OVERTURE

IT WAS the fall of 1987, and I was waiting to be picked up after school when my friend Brett rushed up to me and said, "Dude, you won't believe it! We just got invited to play the Battle of the Bands!" What came next was my first real lesson in leadership—a leadership lesson through the lens of music.

First, we created our shared vision of the outcome: to blow everybody away and win. We chose the songs for our set: two original compositions and two covers (Kiss's "Strutter" and Ozzy Osbourne's classic "Crazy Train"). Next, we organized our ensemble: I would play guitar along with another friend, Will. Brett would play drums and make the crucial contribution of his garage for rehearsals. Then we recruited Mike, an incredibly talented bass player and harmony vocalist, and Robbie, an incredible vocalist.

We rehearsed extensively, both the music as well as our stage show—imagine hilarious kicks and jumps. Hey, this was the eighties after all! Along the way, we coached each other, although maybe a little harshly: "Hey, dude, you dropped the beat. That was lame!" During rehearsals and the performance our fans (read: friends and family) were huge supporters and gave us tremendous encouragement along the way. Finally, the big night arrived, and we gave it our all. We were "baaaaad," which in eighties vernacular meant good.

How did we fare against our competition? Well, although we came second to a more experienced band made up of seniors, we felt on top of the world. The five of us came together to create a shared vision and found connection, purpose, and inspiration along the way. Our band, Onyx, went on to play throughout our home state of South Carolina and developed a strong following. Thirty-five years later, we still have fans who ask us when we are going to play again.

Although I didn't realize it at the time, I learned so many powerful leadership lessons through that musical experience. One thing I learned was that embracing persistence and resilience when you are working towards realizing a vision can be as important, if not more so, than the talent. Onyx rehearsed constantly, virtually every night of the week after school and on weekends. Although we started as the youngest and least experienced musicians in our area, we quickly became the "tightest" (musician lingo for well-rehearsed) band around. We practiced so much, and so loudly, that my amplifier caught fire at one point. (A classic rock 'n' roll move!) Now that's dedication!

And those powerful leadership lessons continued in the musical events that came long after, lessons that would serve me well in my future corporate and consulting careers. Even today, and over the five-plus years that my leadership development firm has existed, "Why music?" is the question I hear more than any other about the framework I use to coach leaders. The context for this question is that my firm, Audira Labs, uses music as a lens through which to teach people about leadership and help them amplify their leadership skills. I started Audira a few years ago after a first act in the corporate world and armed with degrees in philosophy and business. I have a lifelong passion for music, but it's not immediately obvious to people I meet why music and leadership make a sensible marriage. Most often when I'm asked "Why music?" I respond with "Why not?"

There's more to it than that, of course. Music is a universal language that connects us all, regardless of age, family, cultural background, financial position, gender identity, language of origin, geographic location, or worldview. Music has been around since humans could bang rocks together and vocalize, perhaps even before language was formed—and despite being deeply personal, it still manages to unite people. Go to a music festival anywhere in the world and you will likely find a diverse mix of humans connected by magical moments of expression. Music invites and is a platform for creativity and experimentation. Composer John Cage reimagined modern classical music, and Jimi Hendrix revolutionized the electric rock guitar. Sure, there's plenty of unexciting Muzak in the world, but when music is at its best, there is nothing better. And music serves as a natural metaphor for leadership. Extensive studies demonstrate the positive impact that playing music can have on certain cognitive processes such as memory and on specific abilities such as math. Even just listening to music can help your brain and your life in ways that will benefit your leadership skills. But more than just consuming and appreciating, great leaders must create.

You must perform. You must collaborate and harmonize with others. You need to both lead and follow your colleagues, as well as actively listen. You must remain accountable to others and agile and able to improvise. In other words, much of what you do is actually quite musical, or at least it's the same work as that being done day in and day out by musicians. There's a lot you can learn from them, including the importance of cutting loose sometimes and having some fun jamming. For all these reasons, music may be more than just a good way of exploring and transmitting ideas about leadership—it may be the best way of doing so.

There also are numerous examples where we can see links between the world of music and "real world" leadership. In the 1960s, musicians such as Bob Dylan showed us the power of leveraging music to support the Civil Rights Movement and protest the Vietnam War. Beginning in the 1980s, Bono of U2 began working tirelessly to combat poverty in Africa. Most recently, Taylor Swift has led efforts to champion gender equality and the LGBTQ+ cause, to raise funds and awareness for disaster relief, and to fight for voter rights (all while generating revenue similar to the GDP of a small developing nation). These artists see themselves not simply as "creatives" but rather as true leaders with a responsibility for impact.

Before I proceed, let me make clear that this book is for everyone, not just musicians and not only leaders in the stereotypical sense of the word. In the same spirit with which Miles Davis helped to redefine jazz, I'm going to redefine (or "reharmonize," as some musicians like to say) what being a leader means. One thing you'll discover through this process is that regardless of your title, you are a leader right now. Musicians working in their home studios with tiny budgets can become Grammy-winning artists without having a major record label anoint them. Similarly, leaders can make an impact regardless of their title, sector, or path in life.

Another thing you'll discover is that leadership isn't confined to the office. You lead at work but also at home. You lead in the community. To quote my dear mentor, the esteemed Professor Harry Davis from the University of Chicago Booth School of Business, "Leadership is a performance art." The question I'd encourage you to ask yourself is not so much "Am I a leader?" but rather "How will I choose to lead?"

I mean for this book to be a guide—a musical score, if you will—to help you to identify how you want to lead. Maybe you hope to make a career transition, to bring an initiative to life in your community, or to become more effective in your current role. Maybe you want to be a better friend, parent, or citizen. Whatever impact you aspire to make, this book can help you achieve it.

The Path to Audira Labs

My passion for music developed early in life. I was raised in a musical family and started classical trumpet lessons at age twelve. At fourteen, after watching an MTV documentary about rock guitar genius Edward Van Halen (whose name will come up more than once in this book!), I picked up a guitar and have never put it down. As I write this, there are two guitars next to me and five behind me, and there have been times in my life when I've fallen asleep with a guitar in my lap. I began singing, playing piano, and writing songs in my twenties, and I now perform as a singer-songwriter. Thanks to today's digital age, I am on Spotify and your other favorite streaming platforms. I've performed in a variety of bands—my alt-rock group in college was called Delusions of Grandeur—and am working on a second solo album. I have performed at venues across the country and even experienced a European tour (with my high school symphony). I now realize that at every step of this musical journey, I was gaining incredible leadership experience.

As my professional career developed, music sometimes played second fiddle. At Northwestern University I studied philosophy, a subject that, like music, offers various takes on and perspectives of the world. Reading the works of different philosophers sometimes struck me as similar to listening to the works of different songwriters and players in various genres. Perhaps that's why Neil Peart, the drummer from and lyricist for the band Rush, read philosophy on the tour bus. For me, this training proved invaluable as I began my corporate career—first in marketing, then in strategic planning.

During this time, I had the opportunity to work at Shure Incorporated, the global leader of professional audio solutions. Every concert you attend or album you listen to almost certainly involves the company's microphones or earphones. After six years in the workforce, I returned to school to earn my MBA from the University of Chicago Booth School of Business, where I was excited by the school's rigor and incredibly smart fellow students, as well as the opportunity to learn from Nobel Prize–winning professors. This experience lit the spark that would lead me to eventually start my own business.

But before doing that, I held senior global leadership opportunities at Kraft Foods (great branding experience), Digital Innovations LLC (a tech startup, amazing entrepreneurship training), and Weber-Stephen Products LLC (I love to smoke meat, what can I say?). During this time many of my jobs were in product management, which involved listening to customers. I developed a passion for people, specifically for mentoring and coaching them, and for facilitating groups and teams.

By 2017 I was a senior executive with responsibility for leading a large team that I had worked hard to assemble, and I was well compensated. Someone identified me as a person with "high potential" to take on even greater responsibility, so I was assigned an executive coach. My coach and I met to review the results of a 360-degree feedback survey in which my direct reports, peers, and manager had provided feedback on my performance in different areas. My scores were low in some areas in which I thought I should have (and, in fact, thought I was *supposed* to have) scored high—areas such as dominance. Meanwhile my scores in areas that I thought frankly were inconsequential—things like empathy, cooperation, and consensus—were at the top of the charts. At the time, I was feeling unfulfilled for reasons I couldn't quite articulate, so I told my coach that I wasn't sure I was cut out to be a leader.

This experienced kicked off a year-long process of self-discovery, during which time my coach helped me realize that those seemingly unimportant areas of my assessment were superpowers that I could leverage. On the recommendation of a friend, I signed up for a weekend coaching workshop through the Co-Active Training Institute, and with that I found my calling. Ever since then, I've been a certified executive coach and speaker/workshop leader, with a musical twist.

I have no doubt that the qualities that I had discounted—empathy, deep listening, curiosity, cooperation—would have served me well had I remained in the corporate world. In my case, however, the entrepreneurial spark was just dormant. My family has a legacy of entrepreneurship, starting with running blacksmith shops in Europe and moving to helm tannery and plumbing businesses in the United States. I had always wanted to start my own business, but until this point I hadn't put much thought into what kind of business that might be.

That's when Michelle, my wife and business partner, and I sat down at our dining room table and crafted what would become the foundation of Audira Labs. The word *audire* is Latin for *listen*, something I consider a core activity for leadership. We started with a question, as any good philosopher or MBA strategist does: What would differentiate our firm? As much as I would like to take credit for the idea of fusing my career knowledge and experience with a lifelong love of music, I cannot. The suggestion was Michelle's, a testament to the importance of collaboration. She asked a simple yet transformative strategic question: "What would it look like if you integrated your passion for music into this leadership firm?" From there it all flowed quickly: our mission would focus on using the lens of music to amplify leaders through transformational one-on-one executive coaching and experiential team development workshops. Our vision would be to enable a world of deep-listening leaders, and our values would center on curiosity, empathy, and collaboration.

As we built out curriculum and concepts for Audira, I identified numerous parallels between music and leadership, from the importance of listening to the role of performance. We began with a series of experiments that involved launching, conducting, and testing leadership development services—one-on-one coaching sessions and high-impact, experiential, music-infused team workshops—in which participants could apply the concepts of leadership in a unique, compelling, sticky, and sustainable way. Our hypothesis was that people trained in music would likely "get" the concept immediately, and we wouldn't need to work hard to show them why music was the perfect lens for leadership learning.

We were less sure if leaders who were non-musicians would find our services engaging or useful, but they took to it as much as, if not more than, the musicians did. We pulled in musicians as experts to weigh in on how to bring elements of music and musicianship into the office, even hiring a favorite singer-songwriter of ours (Matt Wilson, formerly of the band Trip Shakespeare) to help develop exercises. He currently co-leads a marketing agency called Supervox.

This book is Audira's latest composition. The team and I have had the honor of conducting thousands of hours of one-on-one coaching and team workshops and have supported hundreds of clients ranging from technology startups to Fortune 100 companies, from nonprofit public arts councils to prestigious universities, and from individuals looking to change careers to those reimagining how they lead their organizations. Throughout it all, we have consistently learned as much or more from the leader-participants we have worked with as they have from us. This has been, indeed, an example of creative fusion, and I'm happy to collect the lessons from these experiences in one place.

What Will You Learn?

Together, we will explore a series of key concepts that I believe—and have proven through individual and team case studies—have the power to amplify your leadership. I will guide you through a multipart framework that I have used and that leverages the answers to three key questions: What are my skills and strengths? What are my passions? And what does the world need? If these three questions were circles in a Venn diagram, we'd be looking for the shaded area where the circles overlap, which, using a musical metaphor, we could call our Leadership Anthem.

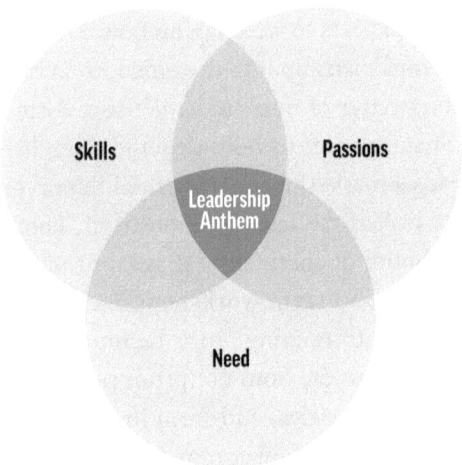

The music-based leadership framework I present in this book all starts with listening (something I will talk about in more detail in chapter 2). To lead, you must listen internally to discover and hear clearly what is most important to you. You must also listen to others and to your surroundings to identify what your team needs most at that moment. From there, I will guide you through what I call the Ensemble Model, a framework that presents a new way of thinking about organizations and leadership. The Ensemble Model has five key roles:

1 **The Composer:** Creates a shared vision

2 **The Conductor:** Strengthens trust, enhances alignment, and builds a collaborative environment in which everyone plays their part

3 **The Performer:** Plays to strengths and maximizes tone, tempo, and volume

4 **The Producer:** Coaches to bring out the best in others while maintaining accountability

5 **The Fan:** Celebrates others

In the coming chapters, I will explore each of these roles. I often draw parallels between leadership and musicianship and will refer to some of my favorite groups and albums. So get ready for some mentions of Louis Armstrong, the Beatles, Miles Davis, Ben Folds, Foo Fighters, Van Halen, Brian Wilson of the Beach Boys, and a few more. If you feel inspired, create a playlist (a mixtape as we used to say) to accompany each chapter. Speaking of playlists, we thought it was only appropriate to provide one for you to enjoy while you explore this book. You can find the link to it in the sources and resources section.

After I teach you the Audira concepts on leadership, I invite you to practice and apply them in the real world. And I would truly love to find out what you're learning. Please email the Audira team and me at info@audiralabs.com.

And now, who's ready to rock?

1
FEEL THE MUSIC
Find Your Heart as a Leader

"One good thing about music, when it hits, you feel no pain."
BOB MARLEY

THE MUSIC WORLD produces an endless stream of love songs. The leadership industry, for its part, produces an endless stream of advice. A conservative estimate of leadership-themed books on sale, new or used, might number in the tens of thousands. You can read about the laws of leadership and levels of leadership, savage leadership and graceful leadership, five-minute leadership and lifelong leadership, Navy Seal leadership and servant-leader leadership. Contradiction, confusion, and cacophony run rampant. If you're searching for clarity in this literature, you might do just as well searching for weight-loss insights in an aisle full of diet books. There is an absolute glut of information.

I love books; that's why I'm writing one. But I recognize that what leaders need is not just one more take on leadership but instructions for how to step away from the whole idea of it and see the challenge from an entirely different point of view. Likely you come to this book with a certain understanding of and experience with corporate hierarchy, as well as some conventional ideas about leadership. But your understanding will be different by the end of it. I see hierarchy as less vertical and more horizontal, with leaders playing a variety of roles within that horizontal structure. This may sound like a radical take, but it's not—I modeled my framework on the music world, where the framework already exists, is in use, and has produced many creative ideas and beautiful, memorable, and inspiring moments and performances. By the time you finish this book, you will see organizations and leadership differently, with the mindset of a musician.

Any fan of live music knows that performances are unique and a little bit unpredictable. A show like Taylor Swift's Eras Tour is a well-oiled machine, and yet there are moments of magic that happen onstage that can never be replicated exactly. A lot of factors go into making those moments happen, and you will learn about these. But before we go any further, I want to reinforce the central role that you—YOU—play in this performance and in the success of your future tour.

The ideas I've developed and collected come from having observed great musicians such as cellist Yo-Yo Ma, known far beyond the world of classical music due to his collaborations with Miley Cyrus, Diana Krall, Bobby McFerrin, and Carlos Santana, among many others. If you've ever seen Yo-Yo Ma perform, it's likely that he was a soloist in front of an orchestra. And if you're lucky enough to see him perform again in this situation, pay attention to his every move, from the moment he steps onstage until he steps off. Yo-Yo Ma looks and acts like the famous soloist that he is. When he sits and prepares to play, he is focused. He maintains that focus as the music swells and ebbs and he digs into his instrument with the bow. The performance isn't his alone: he moves the musicians behind him to meet his level of energy and exactitude. Their response in turn feeds him. The band members of the Grateful Dead had a term for this phenomenon: they called it the X Factor. What emerges transcends rote recital. All the elements in the hall combine to create a shared, enthralling experience.

Yo-Yo Ma's performance is the result of years of practice combined with prodigious inherited ability, but what I want to point out to you is that it also contains heart, a crucial leadership concept for me and one that requires defining. Some people regard heart as equivalent to empathy, and others see it as the kind of courage featured in movies like *Braveheart*. In fact, empathy and courage are yin and yang; the Latin word for heart, *cor*, is even embedded in the word courage.

Heart is closely related to intentionality, a desire and passion for something. It's not enough to use your head or to dress the part of whomever you would like to be. You can think like a leader and even act like a leader but still fail to have a lasting impact. There are countless cellists who wear concert attire, step onto the stage, and play all of the right notes in time with a conductor and orchestra but fail to move people in the way that Ma inexplicably does. Some of that is, of course, due to his colossal talent, but I would argue that an essential component of the magic he creates is that X Factor, or what I call heart.

The great thing about heart is that it's universally held. Every person on this planet has and can summon heart. It is the thing that motivates you. It's the *why* behind your actions. Are you leading because you want to look good?

Because you want to make lots of money? Raise your status? Hold power? Perhaps all of those things are true, but odds are there's something else you are driving towards. The best leaders always start with and embrace a desire. They let it move them. They feel it.

I would love to ask Yo-Yo Ma what he feels when playing music, but regardless of his answer, I can see the feeling on his face. Perhaps music is not what drives you, and that's perfectly OK. Even so, music can help unlock what is most important to you, something that is buried beneath all the plans, ideas, to-do lists, and everything else occupying your thoughts and attention. Music can help to cut through and unlock what's in your heart. At any point while reading this book, take a break, close your eyes, and listen to music. Where does it take you? Use music to tap into what drives you. Listening is crucial in music, and it's just as crucial in leadership. Start by listening to yourself.

Listening is going to be central to your leadership journey, and I want you to keep that in mind as you read. Tap into what you are hearing. Center it. It is what will make *your* leadership journey unlike anyone else's. Your feeling, your passion, your *heart* will be essential to your success. Many people can play the same song, and yet every person brings something unique to their performance. This, heart, is what you bring to your leadership role and makes it unique to you. Everybody has something unique that drives them, and by listening to themselves and others, every single person can tap into that unique force and lead.

Besides our focus on listening, here at Audira we have four guiding principles that I like to think of collectively as a chord—in music theory terms, these principles represent the root, third note, fifth note, and octave. Play them together, and you'll make music. Here they are.

Anyone Can Lead

Leadership has nothing to do with formal titles, status, or positional authority. Nor does it correlate with the number of direct reports, size of a project's budget, or amount of money you make. People may have a senior title (CFO, CIO, CMO, CEO—take your pick) and yet struggle to lead because they fall into the trap of doing what they *think* rather than also incorporating what they *feel* is needed. The best leaders combine both heart and head to make the greatest impact. Many of us are influenced by what we believe our boss, peers, customers, or direct reports expect of us rather than what we believe to be the right thing. In those moments, you aren't feeling much, nor are you doing much to bring anything to life.

Some of the greatest leaders in history initially had little to no formal authority. Mahatma Gandhi, Martin Luther King Jr., and Nelson Mandela did not descend from royalty, graduate from exclusive schools, or operate from positions of unchallenged political power. Quite the opposite: these three all spent time in jail as they struggled to assert themselves. Yet each possessed great vision, relentless passion, and patient dedication that, over time, created change in the world. And they orchestrated this change by inspiring people to follow them. (For a great read on how the best leaders develop such influence over others, check out Seth Godin's book *Tribes: We Need You to Lead Us.*)

In the world of musical leadership, Leonard Bernstein was considered by many to be one of the most important conductors of the twentieth century. He was also a prodigious composer, pianist, music educator, and author. His pioneering artistic impact continues to this day in the Broadway hits that he wrote the music for, such as *West Side Story*, and his leadership of the New York Philharmonic. As if this weren't enough, Bernstein the humanitarian worked tirelessly on behalf of civil rights, protested against the Vietnam War, advocated nuclear disarmament, raised money for HIV/AIDS research, and engaged in multiple international initiatives for world peace.

Anyone can lead if they embody three core elements that all these leaders express: intent, action, and impact.

Intent acts as the compass that points to where we want to head, and why. It consists of our

- values (what we believe)
- mission (why we exist)
- vision (our desired direction)

Intention is a word that's used a lot in leadership circles, and it's the answer to the question "What influence, change, or difference do you want to create?" It embodies a set of *values*, perhaps summed up in a wish or desire. Intention is insufficient without *action*, however. When you have an intention, you need to do something with it. And once you do, assess the *impact* of your actions. Did they work as intended? Did they not?

Think of leaders you admire, and they'll fit this framework of intent, action, and impact. But think outside of the assumed hierarchy. Leadership is not only for an exclusive few tech visionaries, politicians, or social pioneers. You don't need to be a vice president of your organization to lead. If you have intent, take action, and see the through-line to impact, you are leading. That is what it's all about.

Early in my corporate career, I unexpectedly found myself in an unofficial leadership role that proved to be both challenging and pivotal. A colleague had chosen to leave the organization, and my boss asked if I would like (OK, let's be honest, he was telling me) to replace them on a high-visibility cross-functional project team. Although the title that came with the role was nothing fancy (marketing specialist), the opportunity held a new set of responsibilities in which I was interested. What I didn't know at the time, however, was that the role was a critical leadership position, even though it had no formal authority, direct reports, or a budget.

As the entire team was made up of highly experienced technical experts (engineers), I felt out of place and, frankly, outmatched as the only marketing representative on the team. Did I mention I was barely out of college and a liberal arts major? I quickly found myself asked to provide strategic direction to the team members and make decisions that felt far above my pay grade. What did I do? I started from the place I knew best as a musician: I listened. Later on I realized that this role was the place where I began learning the critical skill of leading without formal authority, one of the most valuable lessons ever. You don't need to be officially in charge to lead. You simply need a mindset that allows you to see the path to success.

We Lead in Many Places

We take for granted that we can lead at work. Many of us work for large organizations that require a significant level of management to carry out daily functions. But if leadership stopped at the conference room door, we'd all be in trouble; in fact, leadership manifests itself in small ways, every day, and in every place.

We lead at home with our families as we raise children, support our loved ones, and pass along the values we hold dear through day-to-day actions. We also lead when we listen to the people we love. Listening represents an intent that springs from deeply held values and principles. (I'll have a lot more to say about listening in the next chapter.) But much of what passes for listening is people merely waiting to tee up their next comment. Leaders make sure the people around them are heard (which, interestingly, is just one consonant off from *heart*).

When you coach kids' soccer or softball games, volunteer for a local organization, or serve food at a homeless shelter, you lead in the community. Think again of the intent-action-impact flow. Your intent may be to help address a societal problem, such as food and housing insecurity. You take action by serving food to people who are unhoused, and you then assess the impact you have, whether that's on feeding that day's recipients, supporting an organization that exists to help address that societal problem, or encouraging others to follow your lead. (The recipients and organization may also have an impact on you.) A great example of this in the music world is Adam Gardner, guitarist/vocalist extraordinaire of pop-rock phenoms Guster, who cofounded Reverb, a nonprofit organization dedicated to supporting environmental awareness and sustainability.

We Lead Together

Soon after forming his now legendary band, Jon Bon Jovi realized that he needed a singer and guitar player to complement him. Although Jon was an incredible musician on his own, he recognized that to take his songs to an entirely new level he needed another leader to join him. That choice became the legendary Richie Sambora. (Check out the song "Wanted Dead or Alive" for proof.)

Leadership among teams, families, or social groups isn't a solo activity. I call this idea leadership in the key of Cs: *collaboration* that builds *cooperation* towards a *common purpose*. This leads to *co-creation*.

Leadership requires co-creating with others to build a whole work (in Latin, *opus*) bigger than the individual parts each of us plays. A leader has and shares a vision. A follower is aligned with that vision and through support helps bring it to life. To exist and to accomplish their goals, leaders and followers need each other. Followers can grow into leaders.

The word *ensemble* is typically associated with music, but it's useful in this context too. When you embrace and embody your leadership potential, you bring something unique and powerful to the greater group that changes the dynamic. A charismatic and visionary CEO who struggles with focus and structure knows when to tap other talented players. If they partner with a COO who excels in the areas in which they are lacking, then they have, in the true sense of the phrase, expanded their repertoire. They may also tap people who, though lower on the company org chart, have something to contribute that can't be found anywhere else—a set of real-world experiences, creative abilities, or courage to point out strategic flaws in constructive ways. This CEO's ensemble coalesces around their vision and gives it breath, beat, and life.

We Need to Matter

In my own leadership journey, one of the most important benefits I have received from participating in musical ensembles is a sense that I matter. I have noticed how it feels when I've contributed to creating a set of values, a mission, and a greater vision when writing songs for a new album. I happen to love—and I am good at—ensuring that the ensemble is aligned towards a common set of goals, such as preparing for a big performance. And when we aren't, I can help get us back on track. I feel great when I see how my individual part (playing trumpet, guitar, or piano or singing) plays an important role to the overall ensemble, and that it is especially noticeable when I am not participating. I love helping coach others to perform at their best, and I love how good it feels to support fellow musicians and bands. In all of this, I have always found meaning in participating in something greater than myself.

As leaders, we owe it to those we support to ensure that they feel as if they matter too. Unfortunately, there's an epidemic in corporate America among those who think that their work has little meaning or value and that their roles and contributions are expendable. The Great Recession produced reams of data about this, indicating that employees realized that they felt undervalued by employers and wanted more from life. That led to a Great Resignation: *McKinsey Quarterly* reported that as of August 2021, a whopping 40 percent of employees said they were likely to leave their current job in the next three to six months, with the leading factor being a "toxic corporate culture," rather than a lack of compensation as some might think.

This trend in decreasing employee engagement has continued and has taken different forms, including what has been described as quiet quitting, in which employees essentially check out in different ways, whether that's staying at work while discreetly looking for other employment, or putting in less effort, or changing jobs more often. Unfortunately, many people in the C-suite have not taken steps to change this situation.

But in far more instances, there's a slight space between perception and reality. Just because people believe their work has no meaning doesn't mean it's so. Performing half-heartedly, they still produce positive results, even if those results pale in comparison to what they could be with more effort. What's the magic motivator then? More money? Prestige? A corner office? While perks may seem like the obvious answer, many disheartened workers would rather feel like part of a team.

Adrian Gostick and Chester Elton, organizational culture researchers who have surveyed more than 850,000 working adults over the last two decades, contend that successful companies create a positive, unified culture. In such workplaces, people believe that what they do matters and that they can make a difference.

Companies that create a culture of buy-in defy gravity in their own way. According to Gostick and Elton's survey, these companies boast operating margins that best the competition by more than 14 percent. They retain workers when other companies lose theirs, a huge advantage during the Great Resignation. They also are operating with the knowledge that when one person feels something to be important, that person can bring others along, and eventually everyone is feeling it together. Employees at all levels know that others are counting on them to bring instructions to life. Who, given that kind of freedom, incentive, and challenge, isn't going to rise to the occasion and lead, doing the work to co-create something wonderful and inspirational?

Before we move on, let's revisit my four guiding principles:

1. Anyone can lead.
2. We lead in many places.
3. We lead together.
4. We need to matter.

These four principles are at the heart of what we teach at Audira. They are what motivate and inspire me, at the core of what I do every day. As you progress in your own leadership journey, find out what energizes you. What moves you? What drives you? What is it that you deeply believe and feel? This serves as your premise for all things going forward.

With these foundational principles in place, and through the lens of music, in the next chapter I'm going to explore what is arguably the most important leadership skill of all: *listening*. And, not surprisingly, this happens to be where all musicians and music enthusiasts start their journey.

2

EAR TRAINING

Listen like a Musician

"Knowledge speaks, wisdom listens."
JIMI HENDRIX

LISTENING AMPLIFIES, energizes, and clarifies the thinking of others, and it starts by doing the same for the listener. A good example of this comes from Dave Grohl, the founder and singer of the rock band Foo Fighters, who loves to listen to other musicians (and routinely claims to be starstruck by them, despite himself being twice inducted into the Rock and Roll Hall of Fame). Grohl reportedly attended his first concert in 1983 at Chicago's Cubby Bear club, where he saw the punk band Naked Raygun. What he heard that night energized Grohl in a way he never forgot, and more than thirty years later he brought Naked Raygun's front man Jeff Pezzati onstage at the very same club to perform his punk anthem "Surf Combat." As Grohl explained from the stage, that song was the first punk rock single he ever owned—and hearing it changed his life.

Listening is a concept often discussed in leadership literature, and countless articles proffer ways to help you work towards mastery. In *Harvard Business Review*, Professor Boris Groysberg and research associate Robin Abrahams give nine tips for improving your active listening. In *McKinsey Quarterly*, the now-former dean of Johns Hopkins University's business school Bernard T. Ferrari suggests three different ones in an excerpt from his book *Power Listening: Mastering the Most Critical Business Skill of All*. In *Forbes*, coach Rachel Wells presented her top seven listening-related recommendations.

I've read a lot of articles like these three, and there's one in particular that resonated with me, as it included an observation that I recognized and have observed in almost every musical space I've ever been. It is one that I want to explore before presenting you with my music-inspired framework for leadership.

In 2016, the leadership development consultancy Zenger Folkman analyzed the behavior of roughly 3,500 people in a bid to discover what would help managers become better coaches. Zenger Folkman's consultants used a 360-degree feedback survey, which is an unpopular tool in many corporate environments because it confronts people, sometimes uncomfortably, with their flaws. Yet the exercise produced this finding, which the company's CEO Jack Zenger and president Joseph Folkman described in *HBR*: "Good listeners are like trampolines. They are someone you can bounce ideas off of—and rather than absorbing your ideas and energy, they amplify, energize, and clarify your thinking. They make you feel better not merely passively absorbing, but by actively supporting. This lets you gain energy and height, just like someone jumping on a trampoline."

In describing good listeners, Zenger and Folkman may just as well have been writing about musicians, not managers. Think about a cohesive jazz band: A player listens to their instrument to make sure they sound the way they want to. At the same time, the jazz player listens to other individuals in the band in order to blend and harmonize—and listens to the entire ensemble to hear and understand how all the parts are coming together in the space. All of the musicians in the band are supporting each other, perfecting their shared product through their listening.

What Is True Listening?

I've had the privilege of coaching hundreds of C-suite executives and high-potential leaders, and I have seen how deep, active listening is the most powerful differentiator of successful leaders—regardless of role or industry. As legendary violinist and performer Itzhak Perlman reminds us, "One of the most important elements in teaching, conducting, and performing, all three, is listening."

In music, the first skill many people learn is how to listen through *ear training*, or listening for the connections between the notes, chords, and other building blocks of music. Even young students learn to listen to the pitches in a song and the relationship between them. "Twinkle Twinkle Little Star" begins on one note, and the one that follows it is five steps higher, followed by one that's six steps above the initial note, then five. If that doesn't make sense to you, the odds are you can still sing "Do-Re-Mi" from *The Sound of Music*, which is, essentially, due to ear training.

In many contexts outside of music, our culture emphasizes talking, not listening. Many of us broadcast our every thought and half thought on social media. Doing so seemingly conveys that we are experts, people who have information that others don't. We've been conditioned to talk more than listen, and the awkward silence in a meeting (especially when it's on Zoom) too often compels people to rush in, even when they haven't anything of substance to say. Our minds can become occupied with and distracted by teeing up our next comment as opposed to letting a speaker finish and absorbing what they have to say. From a leadership perspective, this can get us into trouble.

What is true listening, and what misses the mark? Let's start with some examples of what true listening is not.

Hearing versus Listening

Igor Stravinksy, the Russian-born composer widely considered one of the most influential composers of the twentieth century, is said to have once stated, "To listen is an effort, whereas to hear has no merit. A duck hears also."

Hearing is the ear's psycho-acoustic behavior that translates sound waves into electronic signals, which the brain translates into messages and markers. But what's missing here is the step that translates messages into meaning. Think about a recent conversation where the listener may have repeated what you said word for word—but seemed more like a parrot than an active participant. That person heard what you said but didn't necessarily listen.

The Nonstop Talker

My wife and I have a running joke about a heavy metal band from Europe who were famous in the nineties, and for illustrative purposes here will go nameless. They are known for loud, nonstop, and very monotonous songs that we quip "never stop talking" at the listener, leaving us fatigued.

Similarly, some of us may have experienced the friend, family member, or colleague who thinks of themself as a great listener, but rather than listen they talk at length about their listening skills. Extroverts in particular are energized by spending time with others—and by, yes, talking. Passion is a positive attribute in conversation, but only until it robs others of the space to speak and of the opportunity to listen, learn, and interact.

One of my favorite authors, David Brooks, describes the classic listening trap of "topping" in conversations: when one person, after hearing the other person's contribution in a discussion, will immediately respond with something that happened to *them* (and how their experience was somehow bigger or more significant), thereby failing to really listen. This is the reason that the old saying "God gave us one mouth and two ears for a reason" still holds true.

Silence Is Not Always Golden

Many of us confuse true listening with the act of not talking. But the absence of words too often accompanies an absence of presence or connection. In fact, we may be distracted, disengaged, or even daydreaming.

As a musician, one of the most deflating experiences is playing as background music in situations where there is little to no listening by the patrons. I can recall one gig at a brewery at which, after delivering what I thought was a master-class-level performance, the crowd was silent and seemed far more interested in the particular craft beer in front of them. How often do we treat each other like this in everyday professional leadership contexts? I suspect far more often than we'd like to admit.

Nonaffirmations

Yeahs, uh-huhs, and nods: this is what you hear and behaviors you see when people aren't talking. But even a mechanical clown at a carnival can nod its head. When we nod and maybe mutter lukewarm affirmations in tandem, we alert the listener through metacommunication—signals such as our body language, eye contact, and tone of voice—that we're not listening at all. Maybe we're trying to appear courteous and engaged, but the effect is just the opposite.

In *Wayne's World 2*, there's a scene where Wayne Campbell (Mike Myers) and Garth Algar (Dana Carvey) are interviewed by a radio disc jockey. When they start talking, the deejay quickly defaults to canned responses and does other work while they talk. Wayne and Garth notice. "I could say anything right now, like 'You're a complete tool,'" Wayne tells the deejay. "But you wouldn't hear it, because you're a freak with a microphone," says Garth. It's a classic comic scene, but it's less funny when we find ourselves in a situation like it.

Listening with the Intent to Respond (LITR)

LITR is a sinister form of pseudolistening that deceives the talker into thinking that they're truly being heard. This occurs when the listener, as noted above, tees up a response or talking point before the other person finishes their comment. Sometimes that listener jumps in after just a few words. All of us at some time or another have probably done this exact thing. As the late leadership expert Stephen Covey observed in his book *The 7 Habits of Highly Effective People*, "Most people do not listen with the intent to understand; they listen with the intent to reply."

There are several symptoms of LITR, starting with "Yeah, but..." that may represent the fastest way to make a speaker feel unheard. "Yeah, but..." is a surefire way to shut down, attack, or simply bypass another person. It delegitimizes the talker's point and betrays the supposed listener's true intent, which is to appear smarter or more competent than the speaker.

"Oh, that happened to me once" is another symptom of LITR (and an example of what David Brooks describes as topping). This may sound like empathy or positive intent, and perhaps it is an attempt at that. But when you say this, you have either consciously or unconsciously made yourself the center of the conversation. I'm reminded of a discussion I once had with a friend regarding the death of her loved one, during which another member of our party said something like, "I know how hard that is. When my mother died..." and relayed his story. No matter the intent, such a reply, especially in times of grief, communicates a message that the speaker's experience isn't unique or worthy of being the primary focus of the conversation.

And then there's unsolicited advice, which reflects an agenda to fix, manage, control, and problem-solve. Again, the intent is often positive but doesn't represent true deep listening. Think about how difficult it would be for an orchestra or band if the musicians, instead of listening to each other, constantly paused to correct or manage each other's phrasing and playing. The group would never be able to perform.

Most if not all couples (including my wife and I) experience this scenario: After a difficult day or week, one partner shares feeling emotionally exhausted. The other, trying to be helpful, replies with a variation on "Why don't you simply do XYZ?" No wonder the response, spoken or unspoken, is often "I just want you to listen, not fix anything!"

Aside from behaviors that run counter to true listening, there are a few other forces, internal and external, that stand in the way of making you a master listener.

The High-Tech "Noise Floor"

In college, I had the opportunity to intern at several local music recording studios. In return for sweeping the floor, grabbing coffee, and wrapping cables, I got the opportunity to learn the art of music engineering and production. One of the first concepts I learned (aside from listening) was the importance of what is referred to as "maximizing signal-to-noise ratio." Put simply, the idea is to ensure that the desired signal (for example, a singer's melody) is maximized relative to other less desirable signals or noise (such as the microphone hum, an air-conditioning unit, or an airplane flying overhead) that might distract the listener.

Our modern lives include a lot of this ambient noise, and much of it is generated by technology. Several generations ago, there were just three major commercial TV networks on the air, and until 2007, iPhones didn't even exist. In today's digital age, we are continuously bombarded with what feels like an overwhelming amount of technology pulling us in all directions, from calls and texts to social media and video content and now, of course, new generative AI tools. But smartphones, laptops, and tablets make us the most distracted humans in history.

In 2013, three Florida State professors invited students to their lab and observed that simply receiving a phone or text notification significantly hurt their performance on a task that requires attention. And half of the undergraduate students interviewed for a 2019 study in the *Canadian Journal for the Scholarship of Teaching and Learning* said off-task use of technology distracted them from their schoolwork—and this from a generation of digital natives, raised on tech since birth.

Distractions surround us 24/7 in our bedrooms, kitchens, cars, and even our bathrooms, where you can buy wireless speakers and controls that let you play music or heat up the shower water while you're brushing your teeth. It's no wonder that our listening bandwidth now comes at a premium and is too often accompanied by mental exhaustion.

The Need to Be Right and Look Competent

In 1985 the legendary producer Quincy Jones hung a sign above the recording studio for the musicians who would contribute to what would become one of the most legendary recordings of all time, "We Are the World." The sign read "Leave your ego at the door." Jones knew that the biggest challenge of the night wouldn't be artistic capability; these were, after all, some of the best musicians of all time. The real challenge would be the potential risk of egos getting in the way and dismantling the group dynamic that was needed to achieve the end goal.

When our ancestors constantly faced life-or-death challenges, they traveled in tribes for safety and taught children not to wander off alone lest they be attacked by an animal or a rival tribe. Groups provided security and support, and humans survived by learning to be wary of anything that seemed like a potential threat. That survival mechanism is still baked into us.

Even in the twenty-first century we cling to tribes, whether that's your friends, family, or coworkers. No one wants to be unfriended on social media, uninvited to a holiday dinner, or fired from their job. We strive to belong and keep our status in the group. To accomplish this, many of us push our intelligence, capabilities, and competence on people we meet.

Consider the typical corporate meeting or, if you have the occasion to, observe the next one you attend. Beyond the agenda items and words spoken, there's communication of a different sort going on: talking that reveals an emotional subtext through voice inflection, overuse of the "I" pronoun, and some of the behaviors I discussed previously (such as giving advice and LITR). Listen closely and you will often hear

- posturing
- jockeying for favor with upper managers
- shooting down of someone's ideas
- lecturing
- tabling (in actuality, dismissing) someone's enthusiastic pitch for an initiative
- strongly voiced but unsubstantiated opinions

If our ancestors were around to witness this behavior, they might well say, "Yup, that's self-protection. These meeting attendees want to belong. They don't want to be marginalized or forced out of the tribe, and they don't want someone else taking it over."

Listening requires one to open up and, at a certain level, be vulnerable. Tens of thousands of years ago, vulnerability might have spelled death, but there are no woolly mammoths hiding under the conference room table. When you are doing all the talking, you are not allowing yourself to listen meaningfully and may, in fact, be placing yourself in another sort of danger. Someone who monopolizes a meeting might be tagged as a know-it-all by colleagues. Just stop by your nearest office watercooler for confirmation.

Misplaced Priorities

I check in with myself daily for a reminder of what my priorities are and how I can best achieve them. That's healthy. But how many times have you neglected to listen to someone because you have convinced yourself that the task at hand is more important than what they have to say? There's an implied level of self-importance when we say, "Sorry, I'd love to talk, but I'm late to a meeting..." or, "Don't worry, I'm listening while I just check this one text..." Consider how unimportant and marginalized you would feel if the roles were reversed.

Our values must drive our priorities, and listening needs to be a priority or our relationships at work, at home, and with friends will suffer. Children know this at an intuitive level. Parents who pretend to listen, offer unsolicited advice, or allow their distractions to take precedence not only rob themselves of deep, meaningful connections with their kids but set up the next generation to repeat the same mistakes. When you don't listen, it gives others permission to do the same.

The Trap of Cognitive Bias

Effective leaders recognize that active listening enables better decisions that yield stronger outcomes and have greater impact. Put simply, strong listeners avoid falling prey to what psychologists and behavioral economists call cognitive biases. Those include:

- **Confirmation bias:** This is when you listen only to specific inputs and sources. You accept information that confirms what you want to believe and ignore anything that is in conflict with that. For example: "The research is clearly wrong... We must have the wrong focus group respondents." Tragically, confirmation bias tends to drive much of our polarizing political discourse today.

- **All-or-nothing thinking:** This is when you listen in such a way that you believe in an extreme. For example, "I'll either get this job or be homeless."

- **Recency bias:** This happens when you allow more recent events to color your thinking about how frequently something has, or will, occur. For example: "Everyone is talking about how messed up that project is. Just yesterday Bob told me that."

- **Fundamental attribution error:** This happens when you project that something is always a certain way, in every context, based on a limited amount of data. A classic example would be observing someone who cuts you off in traffic. You mutter an expletive and claim that the person is a terrible driver and so must also be a terrible person overall.

- **Saliency bias:** This happens when you fall prey to sensational information and so treat it as more important or more likely to occur. After the 9/11 terrorist attacks, for example, airline travel demand plummeted in large part because consumers were afraid to fly, fearing that their plane might be hijacked. Actual data showed that travelers had a much higher likelihood of dying in a car crash. Tragic and headline-worthy as the 9/11 skyjackings were, they barely moved the needle on the odds of being killed in a plane crash (currently 1 in 9,821) versus in a car (1 in 114).

The Four Levels of True Listening

Up to this point I've talked about what true listening is *not*. But your goal, of course, is to be a good listener, not a bad one. So I'll change key at this point and explore the four modes of listening, as interpreted through the paradigm of music, that will help you move from being a poor listener to a great one.

Mode 1: Tuned Out

In mode 1, listeners are tuned out and indeed out of tune with the speaker. They're absent and distracted from what's going on around them and even from what's going on inside their own heads. Most of us are in this mode more than we care to admit.

Imagine how well jazz trumpeter extraordinaire Wynton Marsalis could perform at Carnegie Hall if he were completely tuned out from his own instrument, his fellow ensemble members, and the audience? As a leader in his domain, he couldn't—and wouldn't. And yet, far too often, this is exactly how many of us who consider ourselves "professionals" find ourselves in different leadership settings. To be fair, often this is not intentional but simply a result of us being distracted, often overwhelmed, and living in a highly noisy world. To combat this, we need to practice the art of tuning in, starting with solo listening.

Mode 2: Solo Listening

In mode 2, as a listener, you begin to tune into yourself and your own instrument, so to speak. Much like a performer listens to their instrument to find the right tone, as a leader, you can listen to yourself to identify your own leadership values. In addition, you can listen for how you are feeling, in terms of your emotions and triggers. You may recognize when you are stressed, anxious, or frustrated, or when a supervisor's demands or an overflow of supposedly urgent emails has triggered an emotional response in you.

In Audira workshops, to illustrate this, we like to have participants (most of whom are not musicians) practice solo listening by choosing a musical instrument and simply noticing the different tones, textures, and expressions that emerge when playing it. We then ask the participants how they might apply that concept to themselves as leaders: What is their metaphorical leadership instrument? How is it unique? What is "their sound"? How might it be adjusted to create different impact in different situations? We get great responses, such as "My instrument is like a drum because I help keep our organization on track!"

Though solo listening is necessary and important, it is by no means sufficient. We must build on it with the next mode, duo listening.

Mode 3: Duo Listening

In this mode, you awaken to what surrounds us. In addition to solo listening (listening to one's own instrument), you also begin to tune into those instruments around you—your friends, family members, and colleagues—and open up to what they are sharing.

A common trap for many people at this stage, however, is LITR (listening with the intent to respond). To combat LITR in team workshops at Audira, we like to have participants practice a musical exercise known as *call and response*, a form that has its roots in traditional African music and is found in blues, folk, gospel, rock, world music, military training cadences, and even in classical music. With call and response, one participant says, sings, or plays on an instrument a short phrase that the listener must repeat exactly. This phrase can start fairly simply and then become more complex as the exercise advances.

What I want you to zero in on is the idea that when you listen to sounds beyond your own instrument, you can tune into others. Call and response helps achieve duo listening.

Mode 4: Listening in Maestro Mode

In mode 4, you combine three types of listening. You listen to yourself, you listen to others, and to cap it off you listen to the space you are in, which means tuning into the room, environment, or context where you are. Few of us do that well or often, but Maestro Mode is where listening turns into leading.

How does Maestro Mode work? You embrace the sound of your own instrument and those of your fellow performers while staying focused on the audience and venue around you. In the corporate world, that might mean listening to colleagues while staying focused on customers and competitors. You are fully present, aware of how everything you listen to builds on itself. Ensemble listening is the hallmark of great jazz quartets and symphonies as well as of CEOs of Fortune

500 companies and owners of small businesses. This is where the most seasoned, practiced listeners live.

It's one thing to define these four modes, but it is another thing to achieve them. In my experience, the most effective listeners practice the following five habits as well.

1. **Unplug:** Digital gadgets encourage us to turn away from what goes on around us. Don't just turn off your mobile device, do it in front of your assembled company. This visual cue communicates to people that you have their full attention. Active listening thrives when the laptop is shut, your desktop is in sleep mode, and the office door is closed. In general, keep interruptions to a minimum. Best-selling author and podcaster Mark Manson recommends a best practice of what he calls putting yourself on a regular "attention diet" from social media and other digital distractions to help maintain energy and focus and be present with others.

2. **Reset:** Before an important discussion, take a few moments to clear your mind of distractions and urgent (or seemingly urgent) tasks. If that's not possible, ask the person you're supposed to meet if they'd be willing to reschedule so that you can be present for them. But be sure to avoid rescheduling with them more than once as that sends a negative message. As a leadership coach, one of the frequent practices I recommend to leaders I support is a "recharging and resetting" practice: before an important call, discussion, or meeting, engage in an activity that adds—not subtracts—focus and energy. This might include a brief walk, meditation, or listening to music.

3. **Engage curiosity:** Sometimes called the "King of Japanese Inventors," Sakichi Toyoda developed a technique of interrogation known as the Five Whys, which would take on

major significance when his son founded Toyota Motor Corporation. The technique is deceptively simple: keep asking why until you get to the root cause of something, and listen closely to each answer so you gain a nuanced understanding of any situation. Sure, asking five consecutive why questions in a one-on-one conversation can sound stilted and strange, but you can leverage Toyoda's technique by responding to answers with successive questions that reflect your genuine interest and curiosity. Also, your questions don't necessarily have to start with the word *why*. For example, imagine that you're talking to a colleague who wants to take up guitar.

QUESTION 1: "Why do you want to learn?"
ANSWER: "I've always wanted to learn how to play."

QUESTION 2: "What made you decide to start now?"
ANSWER: "My son is off to college, and I want to take up something interesting and fun."

QUESTION 3: "How are you going to learn?"
ANSWER: "I'm taking lessons with a music teacher downtown."

QUESTION 4: "Why not take lessons on YouTube?"
ANSWER: "I'm on screens all day at work. I want to have some human contact."

QUESTION 5: "So there's more involved than just music?"
ANSWER: "I already miss my son, and this just seemed like a good way to deal with it positively. Besides, I think I might want to start a band with some guys my age."

Notice how, in the thirty seconds it might take to ask five questions, you arrive at a greater understanding of what learning the guitar means to this colleague. This person doesn't just want to noodle around on an instrument, he wants to connect with someone (and eventually a group of people) now that his son has left the nest. He's looking for a way to fill a void.

The most effective leaders in industries such as journalism, law, medicine, and market research don't succeed because they know all the answers but because they know they don't. They ask questions and open themselves up to learning.

4. **Detach from outcomes:** How many times have you entered into a conversation with an agenda or sensed that the person you were talking to had their own? If this is your starting point, true listening will not happen. Those who master the Maestro Mode know how to remain unattached to a specific outcome and understand that the shared agenda of getting it right beats being right. A great way to check your own level of attachment going into a conversation is to ask yourself, "What do I hope to get out of this discussion?" If your answer is anything other than to learn and/or co-create (for example, your aim is to "convince" or "prove"), you have the opportunity to let go of something.

5. **Practice improv's favorite line:** Improv players learn that staying open allows for endless possibilities. Tina Fey, who started in improv at Chicago's Second City, summed it up like this in her book, *Bossypants*: "The second rule of improvisation is not only to say yes, but YES, AND. You are supposed to agree and then add something of your own."

To practice this habit in a conversation, start by recognizing the other person's point. ("Susan, I love that idea because it will help our team feel more engaged...")

Now, rather than falling into the "yeah, but..." territory, look for your "yes, and..." moment when you feel like you'd like to add to the idea. ("Yes, and one way we could build on that idea is to...")

Fey writes that the first rule of improv is "you are required to agree with whatever your partner has created." And indeed, another way to think of *agree with* terms of active listening is *acknowledge*. We don't judge, correct, or object to what another person says, but instead we strive to *hear it* ("yes") and *harmonize with it* ("yes, and...").

Hi-Fi Listening: Are You Ready?

Wi-Fi is shorthand for wireless fidelity, and hi-fi stands for high fidelity—a phrase rooted in the idea that we hear audio content in all its sonic richness and value. Drawing on this concept, I call the four modes of listening my High Fidelity Listening Methodology (HFLM). When you listen deeply, you stay true to the speaker's intent. What you hear transcends simple syllables and words. You tune into meaning and tune out static, whether from external or internal distractions, just as a hi-fi receiver can lock in on a radio station and bypass the noise on either side of the channel.

HFLM employs multiple senses. You listen with your *ears*, of course, for several things: *Pitch* is what you listen for when you identify the level at which someone speaks. Whether that pitch is high or low can indicate different levels of enthusiasm and passion in a person. *Tone* is also important: A bright, open, and warm tone of voice suggests empathy, compassion, positivity, and support. A darker tone communicates challenges, risks, and problems. *Tempo*, the speed at which someone speaks, is another clue about the speaker's intent. A rapid tempo indicates excitement, urgency, or enthusiasm. Speaking slowly emphasizes importance. And a low *volume* suggests calm, whereas high volume correlates to strong emotion, anger, and frustration.

But you also listen with your *eyes*. Groundbreaking research in the 1960s by Albert Mehrabian, a psychology professor at UCLA, suggested that only 7 percent of communication is verbal, with factors such as body language playing a more important role. Master listeners constantly read body language cues to understand a situation. Expert negotiators, police officers, FBI and CIA agents, and military intelligence personnel are all trained to observe body language. (For more on these and other expert negotiators, check out former FBI negotiator Chris Voss's online MasterClass.)

Now think about these variables in combination. Maestro listeners unlock dimensions of meaning that are otherwise easy to overlook. What might it mean when someone speaks slowly, quietly, and in a low tone as opposed to brightly, rapidly, and at a medium-to-high volume?

Listening also overlaps with *intuition*. How many of us have walked into a room and had a feeling that the energy was tense? Gut feeling is not directly observable with our eyes or ears but on a base level that sidesteps rationalization or overthinking. Our body listens via intuition and picks up on hidden cues, again as a function of the evolutionary advantages that helped our distant ancestors pick up on danger. Remember Harrison Ford's famous line from the *Star Wars* movies? When he says, "I've got a bad feeling about this," you know exactly what he means.

In auditions, musicians are often given sheet music they've never seen before and asked to play it. They have to sight-read, which involves evaluating what's in front of them and running with it. Similarly, Maestro Mode listeners know how to read a room, in that they listen and then perform accordingly. They bring what's unspoken to light and leverage it in the name of clear communication and a more collaborative approach. Their intuition leads to impact.

Putting It All Together

How do you get to Carnegie Hall? Practice, practice, practice. No one knows the exact origin of this famous joke—not even the *New York Times* reporter who tried, in 2009, to find it. But its humor and cheeky wisdom have held true for more than half a century.

No matter your desired destination, you start where you are, wherever that may be. Do your best to tune out static, which may come as the misguided belief that some people are born leaders and you're not one of those people. It's true that because of nature or nurture others may possess advantages that you don't. But in the end, the road to mastery has no shortcuts. It makes equals of us all. And so, you practice. Simply and consistently, practice.

Start by devoting a small amount of time to deeper listening each day. (James Clear's outstanding book *Atomic Habits* outlines how to break down big goals into small increments that build competence and confidence.) In your next interpersonal interaction—be it at home, out with friends, or at work—make yourself fully present. Tune into what you feel in yourself, as well as what you see, hear, and feel coming from those around you. Notice the space and how it might contribute to discord or harmony.

Listening is the core of what I'm going to ask you to do next. It will equip you to assess a situation and figure out what is needed. If you face a challenge at work, you need to listen in order to figure out how to address it. Listening is key to this and to everything we're about to discuss.

MAKE YOUR DEMO

To practice being a better listener, try this: As you engage in different discussions, imagine that a microphone has been placed above your and your conversation partner's heads. Now, as you engage in the discussion, imagine that the microphone automatically points to whomever is talking. Notice how often the microphone is pointed at you versus your partner. Your goal is to maximize the amount of time the microphone is pointed at the other party and to practice Maestro Mode listening. Don't be surprised if you get distracted or get lost in your own thoughts—this will undoubtedly happen! Gently redirect the microphone back to the other member of this duet.

3

THE AUDIRA ENSEMBLE MODEL
The Five Leadership Roles

"The role of the musician is to go from concept to full execution. Put another way, it's to go from understanding the content of something to really learning how to communicate it and make sure it's well received and lives in somebody else."

YO-YO MA

SOME OF the greatest leadership lessons I've learned (besides through music and parenthood!) have come from being an entrepreneur. When I started Audira, I got to do it all: marketing, sales, customer service, operations, HR, accounting, legal, and even shipping. I also learned a lot about information technology. And when I say I got to do it all, a more accurate phrase would be I *had* to do it all. As an entrepreneur, there is often no one else to do these things, so they fall on you—and any volunteers you can recruit to join your cause!

Most importantly, from a leadership perspective, I had to work different modes, as we say in music. Sometimes, I had to be creative and compose things from scratch. Other times, I had to organize and conduct activities. Much of the time, I was executing tasks, performing, if you will. In addition, acting much like a producer does in a music studio, I provided coaching and mentoring to others in our small and growing ensemble to bring out their best. And, finally, I got to stand back and be a fan and supporter of everyone around me.

Reflecting on these different modes of leadership, I developed what we named the Audira Ensemble Model.

By now I've equipped you with five pieces of foundational knowledge: Anyone can lead. We lead in many places. We lead together. We need to matter. And the fifth piece of knowledge is that you need to listen, deeply.

These five principles are like lines on a musical staff. Here's what a staff looks like in what's called treble clef:

In music, these lines are the basis for drafting melodies, harmonies, symphonies, and more. In leadership, you will build on these principles to create your own masterpiece. To do this requires looking at leadership in a new way, which you'll do using what I call the Ensemble Model.

In chapter 1, I talked about the question of *who* can lead (anyone) and *where* they can lead (anywhere). The next logical question is *how* to do this. Once you have your intent, you need to take action in order to make an impact, but what action do you take? You answer this question through listening, which is why in chapter 2 I stressed the importance of deep listening. Before taking any action, you have to take in information. Armed with that information, you can proceed. And this is where the Ensemble Model comes in.

I mentioned earlier that many of us have experience in a vertical hierarchy, in which there's a person at the top of the organization directing everyone else, often supported by senior leaders who have been granted a certain amount of authority. In this traditional paradigm of leadership, there is one (or perhaps there are an elite few) who "leads" while everyone else "follows." Take the idea of that hierarchy and set it aside for now because I want you to envision a different structural model. In this model, everyone leads and does so using five critical modalities based on what is needed for the ensemble to succeed, much like being part of an orchestra, a jazz band, or a rock group. This is the Ensemble Model. If it seems contrary to traditional thinking, that's because it is, and we will explore why it is an ideal framework for leadership.

The Ensemble Model is a significantly different take than many of us are used to. For one thing, in this model, there are five leadership roles: Composer, Conductor, Performer, Producer, and Fan. (I will capitalize all roles we discuss to distinguish these terms from their broader, lowercase counterparts.) And having five leadership roles means sharing responsibility as well as credit. Our current hierarchical system is designed to reward people with the most responsibility, so the Ensemble Model is different in that significant respect.

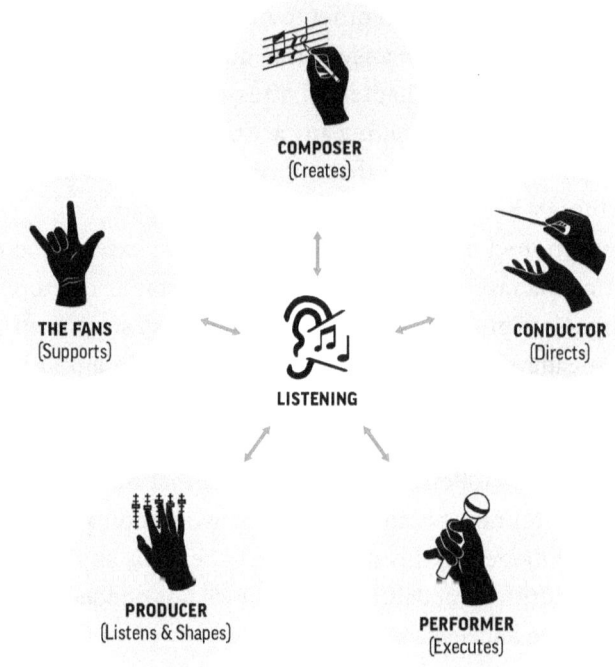

Few offices and organizations recognize an Ensemble Model structure, much less compensate people in a way that recognizes an equal distribution of leadership. Interestingly, in my time both as an employee of and, later, providing coaching for organizations, I noticed how companies would say they wanted employees to "feel empowered to lead" while micromanaging them at the same time. As an employee, the Ensemble Model will enable you to recognize the leadership role you play in a group, lead at your best, and make the maximum impact possible.

If you already have responsibility for managing other people, you will find that the Ensemble Model is a key to keeping people engaged. The Ensemble Model approach enables employees to feel empowered—heard, listened to, and given the chance to contribute. This will naturally help organizations attract, develop, and retain talent. The model helps an organization foster a culture that is supportive, inclusive, and inspiring, and the resulting engagement should improve overall productivity. On the employer side, simply put: this approach will help you keep talented employees for longer and drive growth.

So, what is this novel structure all about? In music, an ensemble is a group of people who play or perform together. It might be a jazz quartet, a chamber music group, a folk band, or an orchestra. The Beatles were an ensemble. Some ensembles, like the Rolling Stones, perform at an extremely high level for a long time and are successful commercial enterprises.

By my definition, an Ensemble, whether musical or otherwise, involves a team of people. That team can be big or small, but what's key is that there are five distinct leadership roles. There is one for the person who has an idea or vision for what to create. I call this person the Composer. There's another role for the person who is responsible for getting everyone to work together towards achieving that idea; that's the Conductor. There's the Performer, who executes the idea brilliantly, as well as the Producer, whose job is to listen deeply and shape the final product. Last but not least, there is a Fan, who supports and cheers on the efforts of the others and provides feedback along the way.

These roles all exist in the music world. Beethoven was a famous composer. Leonard Bernstein, a legendary conductor. Beyoncé's performances bring audiences to tears, and if it wasn't for Quincy Jones's production talents, we wouldn't have Michael Jackson's *Thriller* or Jacob Collier's *Djesse* albums. As for fans, there are millions of them, and we will discuss a few examples in particular to make clear why I consider the Fan to be a role that involves leading just as much as following.

What I've realized is that these same roles exist outside of music, too, even if they haven't been recognized and labeled as such. The premise of this model is that one team needs all of these kinds of leaders. Sometimes you need a person to be visionary and creative (a Composer), and sometimes you need a person to herd cats (a Conductor). Sometimes you need someone to execute a project (a Performer), and other times you need a person to pull the best from their teammates (a Producer) or cheer them on (a Fan).

In the visual, you can see that there is a bidirectional relationship between the five leadership roles and the Ensemble. Conductors, Composers, Producers, Performers, and Fans do not exist in silos. They interact harmoniously to inspire, uplift, and drive the work forward together. And they are always listening to one another for what is needed.

These roles are also not fixed. Say one situation calls for you to act as a Composer. That doesn't mean you are a Composer for life. You can still become a Conductor. A Performer can morph into a Producer. The leadership role you play depends on what is needed for your situation, and you learn what is needed by being an excellent listener. Perhaps you recognized (by listening) that you originally needed a Composer, but after additional listening you realize that what is also needed is a Performer. Still leading, you take on a different role.

The Audira Ensemble Model 55

The roles are fluid, and so is the model. You can be a Composer and then a Fan, or you can be both at once. Let's say you have a three-person team; how can this context with five roles apply? That's easy. One person can occupy two roles. These roles do not define discrete people so much as a set of behaviors. At times you may need to occupy two, three, or even all five of these roles simultaneously. If you're an entrepreneur at the helm of a solo startup, you are Composer, Conductor, Performer, Producer, and Fan all at once, by definition.

Perhaps you find the Conductor role most appealing, and you can easily imagine yourself at a podium directing others. But you don't get to pick just one role and strive towards that. It's all too easy to gravitate to those areas you know best or where you are strongest. Perhaps you're naturally creative and therefore instinctively lean into the Composer role. The problem is that may not be what your team needs at the time. Especially in today's ever-changing economy, it's important to be adaptable.

Over the next five chapters, I will outline each of these roles. Some of the chapters are longer than others, but all five roles are equal in importance. All five are necessary. If I spend more words describing some rather than others, it's mainly because that section has reminded me of something that I want to make sure to cover in the book and the section seems an appropriate space to do so. The main point to understand is that the five roles share authority, power, and influence.

As you learn about each of these roles, I urge you to try them out. That way, when you're in a situation that calls for one role or another, you will recognize what's needed and be prepared to step in and lead to the best of your abilities. Take these roles on tour and practice them in different contexts, even if doing so is at times hard and requires stretching yourself. If you're a natural Composer, what would it be like to be a Conductor or a Producer? Reflect on what role you default to, and then intentionally try a different one.

Just as you stretch yourself, you can help others to do so. If you manage other people (in a traditional structure), what do you notice about your colleagues and what roles they can play? How can you challenge your colleagues to extend beyond their comfort zones?

I don't subscribe to the idea that if you do the four or five things outlined in any given leadership book, you'll be a great leader. I don't even agree with the premise that if you learn these five roles in my own leadership book, you'll be good to go. What I do believe is that you should learn to listen, learn these roles, and learn to practice them. I invite you to experiment—rehearse, if you will—this new and different approach and see what happens. Think of this activity as playing a piece of music that you love but also trying out a new key, tempo, or volume as you do. What impact does the change have on you, your colleagues, or your customers? In time, you will inhabit all five of these roles, at which point you'll be ready to take your ensemble on tour, which I see as the culmination of the Ensemble Model. But before we start planning that, let's first learn about the Composer.

4

THE COMPOSER
Establish Values, Mission, and Vision

"To create something from nothing is one of the greatest feelings. I wish it upon everybody. It's heaven."
PRINCE

I N *THE BEATLES: GET BACK*, the three-part documentary by filmmaker Peter Jackson, there's an extraordinary moment in which Paul McCartney is sitting on a chair with his guitar, killing time as the band waits for John Lennon to arrive for a recording session. But within minutes McCartney is singing the refrain for the Beatles' next hit, "Get Back," seemingly summoned from thin air, and Ringo Starr and George Harrison have joined the jam session. Where did the idea for the song even come from? It didn't exist one minute, and the next it did. But inspiration is accompanied by a practical aspect: once an idea is born and developed, it is then saved to be shared with others.

Composers are like writers working in a different medium. They take a general set of objects that everyone knows, in this case notes, and use those to build music. Their output is varied and crosses all musical genres. Some composers write advertising jingles, and others write masterpieces that outlive them by centuries. But all composition is part theory, part practice, and part inspiration.

The verb *compose* does not refer exclusively to music. One can compose a symphony but also a sonnet. Most children of school age are familiar with those black-and-white-covered composition books with lined pages ready to be filled with their thoughts. *Merriam-Webster*, under the entry for compose, states also "fashion," "constitute," and "produce." But implicit in each of these actions is the idea that something is being given meaning and shape, and the person doing that work is the composer.

The composer is not necessarily the person on stage—although one can, like McCartney, be both a composer and performer—but the person upon whose composition the performance is built. To understand the distinction, think about country star Dolly Parton, a brilliant performer with equally if not more brilliant songwriting (composing) abilities. One of her biggest hits, "I Will Always Love You," was written in the same time span as another winner, "Jolene." According to the *Guinness World Records*, "I Will Always Love You" is the hit with the most consecutive weeks at number one on the United States singles chart. But the female solo artist referred to is not Parton but Whitney Houston, who recorded the song for the 1992 film *The Bodyguard*. After all, a composition doesn't belong solely to the composer; a performer can build upon it, and "I Will Always Love You" is a case in point. Houston's rendition took a song that was already a hit in the country music world and broadened its audience.

The Composer takes an idea, molds it, and turns it into something concrete for a team. In a non-musical situation, the Composer creates something for others to build on, which could be a mission statement or a more detailed plan of action. Ted Turner (not the English guitarist of the 1970s, but the businessman who founded CNN) is a Composer, as described by his onetime colleague Jim Crupi, who was a pre-founding strategist for CNN. In a 2016 article titled "What Great Leadership and Music Have in Common" (a premise I wholeheartedly endorse), Crupi wrote that "a leader is both a singer and a songwriter." And about Turner, he wrote, "He's the company's founder and is looked at by everyone as the person in charge... [But] he focuses on their values and their commitment to excellence. It is the music of his leadership, and it is subtle but powerful." Turner didn't just create CNN; his vision of a twenty-four-hour news channel transformed the media landscape.

As a Composer, you don't need to aspire to become Paul McCartney, Dolly Parton, or even Ted Turner. The point is to recognize that the mission, vision, and values that guide a team originate with your role as a Composer. And to be a successful Composer, you need to ask yourself a few important questions.

Who Is Your Audience?

In 1991, the world was taken by storm by a to-that-point unknown band, Nirvana. Introducing the world to "grunge" music—a counter to the highly polished music of the

1980s—Kurt Cobain and the band connected powerfully and directly with their audience: those who, like them, felt disenfranchised and left out of mainstream society.

When we think about history's famous composers, we may be tempted to ascribe their success purely to their genius and innate abilities. But the fact is, artists need to eat, and composers have always had patrons they've needed to please. That audience factor is not unimportant, and I would argue that it's actually crucial to many compositional successes.

In chapter 2, I told you about how the centrality of listening is not just about physically hearing but about taking in and interpreting the reactions of other people. Along these lines, when they create, many master composers are constantly listening to—and thinking about—their audience. Take John Williams, who composed the music for many movies including the first three *Harry Potter* films, *Home Alone*, *Jurassic Park*, *Jaws*, and *Star Wars*. Williams's scores match the underlying cinematic material brilliantly. His sawtooth, two-note melody will be forever associated with a blood-thirsty shark, and his curtain-raising regal fanfare transporting us to a long time ago in a galaxy far, far away will likely reign among the most famous musical riffs in history. When Williams receives a commission and prepares a score, he could go in myriad directions but is guided by the script and the audience's anticipated reaction to it.

As leaders in an ensemble, you need to think about your audience and Compose accordingly. What do your customers value? What do they need? What motivates them, and what motivates your colleagues? Composers should consider the audience before setting down the first notes.

What Is Your Intended Impact?

The best composers across a spectrum of genres—whether classical, jazz, rock, or R&B—begin with the end in mind and think about the place they want listeners to land. Music is a form of expressive storytelling, and the composer is the storyteller. When he was spinning "Get Back" out of the blue, Paul McCartney didn't know exactly where he was going, which is part of why watching his conjuring is so magical. That said, he had a strong sense of who was in his audience and what kind of songs those people responded to. Even at that moment, in the artificial environment of a studio, he knew that audience well enough to be able to write for it and with a desired impact in mind.

In your ensemble, once you've identified who your audience includes, ask yourself what you envision for them. If your main audience is customers, how do you want them to feel when presented with a new product or process? If you're hiring an employee, how do you want to welcome that person?

When laying out a vision, a Composer needs to consider three important factors. First, consider the *why*, which is what you are hoping to achieve—or the reason for your composition. What do you want your audience to learn or take away from an experience? What's important? As author and inspirational speaker Simon Sinek says, "Start with the why." Sinek contends that when you successfully telegraph the passion behind the why, you connect and communicate with the limbic system of the listener's brain, which governs their behavioral and emotional responses.

Second, consider feelings. In many corporate leadership settings prior to the Covid-19 pandemic, "feel" was a four-letter word. In general, success was measured by shareholder returns and other performance indicators. Only after employees started leaving en masse in pursuit of greater fulfillment did the pendulum swing and employers adopt a different tone. Recently I have seen more companies, and specifically more employees responsible for talent acquisition, acknowledge issues such as mental health. Employees need to feel engaged, inspired, and supported, or they will leave, and the single biggest competitive advantage a company has is talent. Indeed, feelings have become an economic variable for employers.

In my view, there's no escaping that humans are emotional creatures, and we must recognize the important role that feelings play in behavior. How do we want our audience to feel as a result of our composition? Is our message one of loss and recovery? Of urgency and the need to act? Of hope and possibility? In the corporate world as well as in the artistic one, messages that recognize emotions go a much longer way towards motivating, moving, and inspiring people.

Lastly, consider action. As we learned in chapter 1, leadership is composed of equal parts intention and action. As a Composer, ask yourself: "What is my end goal? What do I ultimately want my audience members to do?" (Start your work by thinking not only about what your audience wants from you but about what you want from your audience.) In music, the end goal might be to get your audience on the dance floor. Perhaps that's what Antônio Carlos Jobim was aiming for when writing bossa nova songs such as "The Girl from Ipanema." The rock band Rage Against the Machine has not been shy about wanting to spread its political views and messages, such as a desire to free prisoner and activist Mumia Abu-Jamal. Bob Marley advocated for peace and pan-Africanism (and that is an admittedly simplistic summary of his full, complex life and views).

The Composer's Steps

In chapter 1, I talked about the importance of a leader's intent and how that manifests in an organization's values, mission, and vision. These leadership terms—values, mission, and vision—can be correlated with the musical terms tone, harmony, and melody, respectively. All three are applied by composers in the musical sense and should be applied by Composers in the leadership sense.

Express Your Values in Your Tone

In step one, composers think first about the overall *tone* of the piece they're writing. Will it be warm? Bright? Edgy? What mood does the composer want to create? That will affect any number of their other decisions, such as what instruments to include and the tempos of the piece.

There's a parallel to this in leadership. In a traditional strategic planning perspective, the values of an organization represent the answers to the questions: What do we believe? What do we value? And how do we wish to lead? In answering these questions, the Composer establishes the primary values that govern how a team or organization operates. For example, the leader as Composer might want to leverage empathy in the organization in the same way a music composer might want express a warm tone in the music.

However, just as one piece of music can lean into different tones, so, too, can an organization emphasize different values at different times. Is respect a core value for your organization? How about integrity, accountability, trust, empathy, and passion? Obviously, all of these values are desirable at some point. That said, a Composer needs to maintain a certain focus that will guide other tasks and activities.

Mission to Harmony

When writing a piece of music, the Composer considers *harmony* in addition to tone. There are countless potential note patterns that could fit together to form chords and chord progressions to create multiple harmonies. One textbook harmonic sequence common in Western music is known as I-IV-V. If a song is in the key of C major, the sequence of chords would start on the first note of the scale, then the fourth note, then the fifth—so C-F-G. Many pop songs have their roots in the same chord progressions. Bon Jovi's "Living on a Prayer," Cyndi Lauper's "Time after Time," and Bruno Mars's "Grenade" all utilize the I-V-vi-IV progression, three major chords interrupted by a minor one.

In the leadership world of composing, harmony translates to the idea of your mission. Within the arena of strategic planning, an organization's mission answers the questions: Who are we? Why do we exist? And for whom do we do what we do? Much like a compositional harmonic structure in a song, the mission is the basis for everything an organization does. At Audira, our stated mission is to enable leaders, teams, and organizations to amplify their leadership. Our mission articulates why we exist and for whom.

A Melody of Vision

The third step is *melody*, the sequence of single notes that is overlayed on top of a chord. The melody is what you sing along with, or whistle along with if your voice needs a break. If I were to ask you to sing "Let It Be" by the Beatles, you would almost certainly deliver the melody. In strategic planning parlance, an organization's vision articulates what the company wants the future to look like and its associated impact. Similarly, in a composition, a melody tells a story to the listener in much the same way.

Just as a composer spins a melody out of notes, a Composer articulates a vision or the desired impact of the organization. Bill Gates had this vision: "A computer in every home, running Microsoft software." More than three decades later, it's safe to say that his vision was largely achieved; we all are familiar with computers, just as we are familiar with the lyrics and melody for "Let It Be."

These three things—values, mission, and vision—together guide and inspire others in the Ensemble. But when you have all three, are you finished? The answer is no because the job of a Composer never ends. When a composition is complete, the Composer has an opportunity to listen to it and see how it takes shape in the hands of the Conductor, Performer, Producer, and ultimately the Fans. After an initial listen, they may decide to make additional tweaks to the composition. And after that, the Composer also has a responsibility to continue creating and composing, to dream up what comes next.

When I was at Shure in the mid-1990s, I had the opportunity to work on a groundbreaking new wireless microphone system for professional musicians and sound engineers. Throughout the project, we regularly solicited customer feedback using prototypes to see what they liked and what they wished to see improved. At one point, a customer made an offhand comment saying, "The system you've designed is great, but what I really wish I could do is to somehow control it remotely, far away from the stage or even a different location entirely, if I'm not at the venue. I know that's science fiction stuff, so I'm sure that won't happen."

With this inspiration in mind, our project team set about the task of composing: how might we create a feature that would allow the user to remotely monitor and control the system, thereby increasing convenience, confidence, and ease of mind? After extensive brainstorming, we identified what was truly innovative at the time: using a computer LAN network to allow the user to remotely monitor and adjust settings from anywhere with an easy-to-use software program and network interface. When we introduced this feature, it immediately helped make our product a market leader.

From a leadership compositional perspective, although we wouldn't have used these phrases necessarily, we had our tone (values), harmony (mission), and melody (vision) in place. Our tone came from our core values of customer focus and, specifically, listening. Our harmony came from our consistent mission to enable our customers' confidence through a reliable and quality solution. And our melody was oriented around being the most trusted brand in audio for our customers.

Just as anyone can lead, anyone can be a Composer. Perhaps you work in a corporate environment and report up through several ranks to a CEO who is responsible for setting the company's course. It may be your instinct to believe that everything covered in this chapter is most relevant for a CEO, but that isn't the case. Remember the example of Leonard Bernstein I offered in chapter 1: his work as composer didn't stop him from conducting and performing too. Regardless of your role in the hierarchy of an organization, you can be a Composer and create a mission and vision for yourself.

Here are just a few thought-starters of what leadership composition might look like:

- creating a new project, product, process, service, initiative, group, department, or organization
- supporting a new customer or market

- initiating any creative, volunteer, or community-based endeavor such as an article, book, video, song, podcast, performance, charity drive, nonprofit board, or mentorship

Who is your audience? What are your goals? Anybody can be a Composer. Give it a try.

MAKE YOUR DEMO

To practice being a Composer, experiment with using your High Fidelity Listening Methodology skills. What do you hear that is needed? Maybe a family member needs support, or a customer has a need, or a member of your community is underserved.

On the basis of that need, try composing a leadership solution using the concepts described in this chapter (such as I demonstrated with the example of my work at Shure). Don't worry about creating a perfect composition. As it is often said, perfection is the enemy of progress. As you're composing, ask yourself: "What might be possible with this composition in place? What impact might it have?"

5
THE CONDUCTOR
Create Space for Others to Succeed

"The real art of conducting consists in transitions."
GUSTAV MAHLER

ANYONE ATTENDING their first orchestral concert can figure out pretty quickly who is in charge. After the orchestra is seated, the head violinist comes out to lead the orchestra in tuning. But then after the head violinist comes the conductor, who acknowledges the audience with a bow or head tip before taking the podium. They then turn to the orchestra, raise both hands, and signal the start of the music.

I happen to live near Chicago, home to Orchestra Hall and the great Chicago Symphony Orchestra. The CSO has had only ten music directors (conductors) in its history, and a recent trip illustrates why some have been so revered. During a recent season the orchestra played *Pines of Rome*, an incredible tone poem completed in 1924 by the Italian composer Ottorino Respighi. Each of the four movements (sections) of this piece are an auditory description of a different area of the Italian capital. The last movement summons the Appian Way, and the CSO transported the audience to that ancient military road. The movement started with beats on the timpani, and soon woodwinds, strings, and brass flowed in, all making you feel as if you were marching down the Appian Way. Under conductor Riccardo Muti, the entire orchestra moved in sync to the piece's spectacular conclusion.

The Conductor is the second member of our leadership Ensemble, so let's take a moment to understand what that means outside of an orchestra hall. Just like Muti, the leader as Conductor gets people in a group to work together, marshalling resources and talents into a cohesive whole. Individual Conductors have their own ways of doing this, but communication is central to creating alignment. Some Conductors manage to transmit and literally conduct energy to create a circuit of inspiration between team members.

But what exactly is the job of the Conductor? Well, I see as it as having five main tasks.

Create a Safe Space

In recent years, the phrase *safe space* has taken on political overtones, but it originally emerged from the discipline of psychology and refers to the creation of supportive environments where people can express their thoughts and identities without judgment. In corporations and human resources departments, safe space has come to mean a place where an employee can speak up and raise concerns without fear of reprisal.

In the Ensemble Model, a Conductor starts by creating such a space where team members feel supported so that they can perform. This may mean making sure the office is comfortable (not sweltering, but not freezing either) and ensuring colleagues feel physically safe and adequately motivated. Even Yo-Yo Ma is unlikely to offer his best interpretation of Bach's *Cello Suite in G* if the room where he performs doesn't help him to feel comfortable, let alone inspired.

This seems so basic, and yet too often many of us encounter scenarios in which employees lack physical, mental, or emotional safety. Situations involving sexual harassment, mental health discrimination, and corporate cultural toxicity occur more frequently than we'd like. Many of us have likely experienced these situations in some way or know colleagues who have. Listen to your team members, whether they are bandmates or corporate colleagues, and figure out what a safe space means for them. In what kind of environment will they feel most comfortable, creative, valued, and inspired?

As you do this, consider their working location, environment, and time. For a musician, the workplace is typically a stage, rehearsal room, or studio—and those can at times feel inadequate. Edward Van Halen felt so strongly about the place he worked that he built his own studio to gain more control over his recording process. In this sense, he conducted himself and his band and created an environment that supported and maximized the value of their creative process.

For many of the rest of us, our workplace is an office defined by, among other things, desktop computers and traditional work hours. The Covid pandemic brought into focus an issue that employees have wrestled with for years: workplace flexibility. As pandemic restrictions have faded into history (one hopes), our world has started to slowly return to a sense of normalcy (perhaps a new or different form, at least), leaving employers with an opportunity. After the pandemic, many leaders who demanded a return to "business as usual" provoked widespread backlash of staff resentment and accelerated employee-led departures. No single approach fits every situation, which is why it's important to listen carefully and allow for flexibility where appropriate. If you're a manager, ask your team members whether they prefer working from home or the office, or in some combination. Do they work best in the morning, afternoon, or evening? My former employer Shure Incorporated is among the companies that has transitioned to a "work from anywhere" policy, which has enabled it to tap into a larger pool of potential talent.

A safe space also implies a high degree of security. To what extent does the team or organizational culture allow—or, even better, promote—debate, disagreement, and speaking up? Do your team members feel that they place their jobs in jeopardy if they voice concerns? A company that encourages free expression one minute and punishes it the next puts a damper on morale, and employees may be reluctant to point out the hypocrisy. For a better model, consider Abraham Lincoln, who after his 1861 induction appointed to his cabinet three onetime challengers for the presidential nomination: William H. Seward as secretary of state, Salmon P. Chase as secretary of the treasury, and Edward Bates as attorney general. The wisdom of this decision—laid out by Doris Kearns Goodwin in *Team of Rivals: The Political Genius of Abraham Lincoln*—bore the mark of a great Conductor: Lincoln created a space where even his fiercest critics could speak candidly.

As a final element of safe spaces, consider systems, processes, and resources. How many times must people try to do their work with insufficient tools to succeed? Try asking a lead clarinetist to play *Pines of Rome* with a broken reed. Can they do it? They will try because they are a professional. But will they perform at their highest level? Absolutely not. Ask your team members what they need to excel. Their needs could be anything from the ergonomic to the electronic, digital to architectural. Would sun-filled rooms and inviting communal spaces raise productivity? It's worth asking the question.

Your team members may look to you to see what behavior you demonstrate and how far you will go to keep them happy. As a Conductor, you don't have to give employees every last thing they ask for, but you honor your team when you empower its members. Be honest about any time and budgetary constraints, and then brainstorm solutions and invite creativity.

Foster Connection and Community

The best Conductors shape a process for community-building. We are social creatures who crave—and require—human connection. From the London Philharmonic to the Rolling Stones, the conductors helming these groups have worked to foster environments in which performers, crew, and countless audience members have felt part of a larger community. You have the same responsibility where your team members are concerned. Here again the pandemic proved instructive. Think about how many of us felt disconnected from family, friends, and colleagues and how this impacted our mental and emotional well-being. Between August 2020 and February 2021, the number of adults with anxiety or depression symptoms (as measured over seven-day intervals) jumped from about 36 percent to over 41 percent, according to the Centers for Disease Control and Prevention.

One way a Conductor can enable and activate connection for the other people in our Ensemble is through meetings—or rehearsals in my musical metaphor. As basic as this may sound, a regular cadence of meetings is critical. As an executive coach, I often hear leaders say that they rarely or inconsistently convene with their manager or team. Some leaders shy away from meetings, knowing how much employees despise them—and for good reason given how many bosses blather on endlessly. Meetings need purpose and clear objectives. When in doubt, call to mind the picture of band members working to listen to each other and collaborate on larger goals.

As you work out the rhythm for your meetings, consider the framework I use:

- one-on-one meetings—weekly
- team meetings—every two weeks
- project meetings   monthly
- career and strategic-planning meetings—quarterly
- ad hoc—always helpful; just avoid these becoming a substitute for regular gatherings

Make your meetings matter. If you need to make some collective decisions, share updates, or brainstorm and harness the group to solve a problem, then schedule a meeting. But if you don't have anything to meet about, don't meet. Your team will thank you, whether overtly or silently.

When you do meet, choose your communication platform wisely. We have more virtual venues for connection and collaboration than ever before, allowing us to overcome the constraints of location when in-person options are insufficient. Some of these are unmatched for speed and convenience, and yet they come with potential pitfalls—just ask anyone who has hit send on a note to the wrong person or fallen victim to an unfortunate word choice via autocorrected dictation.

Consider which platforms, and what mix of them, will work best for your Ensemble. Here are some that I've ranked in terms of most to least effective:

- face-to-face interaction, either in an office or work environment or at an outside location such as a coffee shop, a restaurant, or hotel boardroom (employees often see an outside location as a safer space)
- video calls through platforms such as Zoom or Microsoft Teams
- audio conference calls
- messaging apps/channels such as Slack, Basecamp, or Trello
- email or text

Confident Conductors know that smaller groups facilitate stronger connections. Musically, these groups can take the form of duos (two players), trios (three), quartets (four), and sections (composed of wind instruments, brass, percussion, etc.). From a leadership perspective, you can take inspiration from these musical groupings as you help your team members to thrive via the right interpersonal dynamic.

Identify opportunities for members of your team to find a mentor, separate from their manager, or an executive coach who can serve as a sounding board, offer perspective, and share counsel when appropriate. You could also create accountability partners or pods, small groups of two to five individuals who choose to meet on a semifrequent basis to support one other in staying on track towards achieving their respective goals. You can help your team members select and form these small groups by identifying prospective pod matchups who share complementary skills or combinations of people who would encourage positivity and possibility thinking (a growth mindset that prompts people to embrace opportunities).

Expand Communication and Collaboration

Conductors perform at their peak when they inspire the players around them to perform at their best. It's not easy to get an Ensemble of people with divergent skills and approaches to collaborate and work towards something bigger than themselves, but for the leader who thrills at the prospect of making a meaningful impact and ultimately leaving a fruitful legacy, there is no higher reward. Daniel Burnham, the architect who coauthored the 1909 *Plan of Chicago* and would later contribute to city plans for San Francisco, Cleveland, and Manila, said it well: "Make no little plans; they have no magic to stir men's blood and probably themselves will not be realized."

In 1985, Quincy Jones and Michael Omartian fully inhabited the role of Conductor when they assembled a varied panel of performers including Bob Dylan, Michael Jackson, Cyndi Lauper, Willie Nelson, Bruce Springsteen, and a few dozen more for a performance of the song "We Are the World." Jackson and Lionel Richie wrote the song that was recorded on one night to raise money for African famine relief. Inspiring all these people with their different vocal styles to harmonize together represented a triumph of heart and the Conductor mentality and is a pinnacle of all-star achievement in music.

As leaders, you have a responsibility to ensure that your players coordinate and see beyond their individual efforts. To support this, as a Conductor you can align people's objectives by using the RAISE framework (as in, raise the baton).

R **Receive:** Does your team Receive the necessary tools to live your shared values, mission, and vision? This can't be emphasized enough, but many leaders and teams are improperly resourced and then told to do more with less. What does your team need to perform at their best?

A **Alignment:** Are they in Alignment with the values, mission, and vision of the organization? Have you given your team members the opportunity to provide input in a way that supports your shared goals? Or are they simply being told what to do and expected to get on board?

I **Inspire:** Do you Inspire your team's desire to live out the organization's values, mission, and vision? Even with all other elements in place, Conductors have a charge to inspire the desire. In his now famous TED Talk, conductor Benjamin Zander illustrates the inspiring power of classical music and, in so doing, demonstrates his own natural inspiring impact, mesmerizing the audience. As a Conductor, your role is to communicate your intentions clearly. The other Ensemble members will ultimately choose how much they engage with the task, but they look to you for inspiration.

S **Speak/Share:** Do you Speak/Share a common vocabulary? How do percussionists communicate what they need from the string section, and vice versa? How does a computer engineer communicate ideas to a sales manager when it may seem like one speaks French and the other Greek? In the name of effective communication, Conductors must forge a common vocabulary across different parts of an organization. The aviation sector offers an excellent benchmark for this. Both commercial and military pilots and other crew members, regardless of role or branch, are trained with the same vocabulary to avoid confusion in high-risk situations. Consider how you can implement a more effective, simple, shared communication framework for your team.

E **Embrace:** Does your team Embrace the values, mission, and vision? Most challenges and issues with strategic alignment start and end here. Managers often have trouble expressing what's most important to their organization in a way that individual employees can understand. Vague platitudes about shareholder value and putting quality first fail to inspire people. One company that does this exceptionally well, in my opinion, is KIND Snacks. Their brand and organization has a clear and compelling statement of purpose: creating a kinder and healthier world—one act, one snack at a time.

Right People, Right Seats, Right Time

When Brian Wilson was writing the Beach Boys' 1966 album, *Pet Sounds*, he knew exactly what instruments and performers he needed for each song. At the time, it was unheard of to integrate wind, brass, strings, percussion, and other "noncontemporary" instruments into pop or rock songs. But by doing just this, Wilson established a benchmark against which rock albums would be measured for decades to come.

Though some people might rank the Beatles album *Sgt. Pepper's Lonely Hearts Club Band* as a greater achievement, Paul McCartney has stated in numerous interviews that he derived a significant share of his inspiration for it from listening to *Pet Sounds* for its innovation and creativity. For example, the song "God Only Knows" employs twenty session musicians playing instruments including French horn, sleigh bells, clarinet, harpsicord, twelve-string electric guitar, and, for the first time in pop history, orange plastic juice cups! The vocal harmony rounds in the coda represented another uncommon technique for 1960s pop. And the word *God* had never been used in a pop song title, largely because it was considered taboo.

But one decision Wilson made trumped those innovations. Instead of singing the lead vocal, as he had done on earlier studio versions, he asked his brother Carl to do it. To this day, "God Only Knows" is considered Carl's best lead vocal performance and is an outstanding example of what happens when you put the right person in the right chair at the right time. Wilson's album wasn't the result of a lightning strike, or even of happening to have the right people around at the right time. Rather, he engaged in some serious organizational planning.

When planning, it's crucial to hire the right candidate. One of the most important aspects to consider when you are inviting a new member to join your group is *fit*. In this case, I'll define a fit for the organization as an alignment with the needs of the individual, the overall Ensemble, and the audience. After all, you probably wouldn't want an acid jazz guitarist, no matter how accomplished, in a synth-pop band.

A former mentor and CEO once broke down for me his assessment process, explaining that he uses three simple yet effective questions when evaluating a candidate to bring into his team or organization. First, he said, can this person teach us something new? This question goes beyond the scratched up old lens of asking whether they have the necessary skills for the position. Instead the question probes what skills, knowledge, or expertise the interviewee could bring to the Ensemble to help it grow and innovate. I love that this approach speaks to an organization that stresses a culture of learning.

Second criterion: Could he imagine sitting on a fourteen-hour plane ride with this person and still want to work with them? Simple and amusing, yet profoundly pragmatic, this question marks an original way to evaluate collaborative ability and overall cultural fit.

Third, is this person passionate? We all lead at our best when we embody passion. But an individual doesn't need to be enthusiastic about all aspects of a role or organization to be considered passionate. In fact the lesser-known meaning of *passion* is "to suffer for what you love," which probably resonates with anyone who has had to deal with many urgent but unimportant requests, red tape, and other potential time wasters. Yet it's passion that sees the best people work through those barriers, the promise of greater rewards for a job well done. This is as true for the people in the C-suite as it is for the candidates worth hiring.

The Conductor is responsible for working with the Ensemble to identify where an individual's skills and passions align, and then placing that person in a role that addresses a need. If you are planning to put people in the right chairs at the right time, you need to find overlap between the three

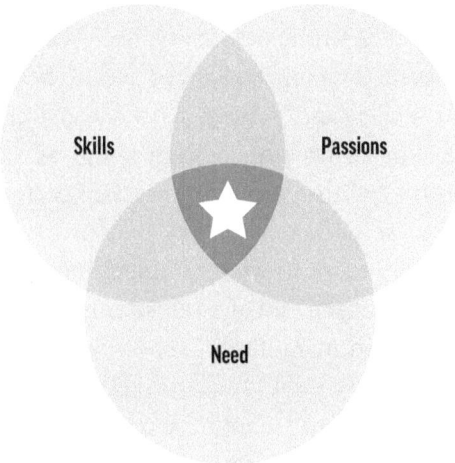

circles as illustrated in the graphic that I shared with you in the "Overture" of the book. But what happens when these circles don't overlap? What if you tap someone for a task who excels at it but no longer loves it? Or deploy someone who has a passion for a role yet lacks the necessary skills? Or find a person who possesses skills and talent but in an area for which there is no current need in your organization? Let's explore two examples: one musical and one leadership-based.

My oldest son, Jonah, started playing the oboe in fourth grade. While he enjoyed it for many years (and still does), he started to become bored around ninth grade. He excelled at the instrument, but it didn't grab him like it first had. His band director encouraged him to try out for marching band, which doesn't typically need oboe players but does have saxophonists. He specifically suggested that Jonah try out on tenor sax. The director had a need for tenor saxophonists in marching band, and he recognized that Jonah had a passion for learning new and challenging things. And Jonah had a skill set developed from years of playing the oboe. Oboe players, familiar with reed instruments, can typically learn saxophone quickly. The band director recognized overlap between need, passion, and skills, and playing with the marching band became one of Jonah's favorite pastimes. And, as it happened, learning the sax led him to another passion: performing in a jazz ensemble.

This happened to me as well. As I mentioned at the beginning of this book, at the end of 2017, after nearly twenty-five years of working in marketing, I felt unfulfilled. With the help of an executive coach, I recognized that I had untapped passions for coaching and mentoring others that I could integrate with my marketing skills to fulfill my need for leadership development. This recognition helped me forge a new career path in executive coaching. What's more, my wife Michelle's observations helped me to integrate my love of music into the art of leadership coaching and team development.

As Conductors, you can achieve uncommon results when you honor the value, mission, and vision of the organization (as laid out by the Composer); recruit the right Ensemble members; assign them to the most appropriate roles; and deploy those members strategically to accomplish projects, initiatives, and other goals. But the most effective organizations tie long-term strategies to the talent and skills needed to position those organizations for future success. This requires creating succession plans for all parts and levels of the organization.

Whether you're the CEO or a manager, ask yourself what succession planning look likes for your team or yourself. Countless case studies have examined what happens when organizations fail to properly prepare themselves for personnel departures, the classic example being General Electric before and after the retirement of Jack Welch in 2001. By 2021, GE stock had lost close to 80 percent of its value. Ironically, Welch had said in 1991, "From now on, [choosing my successor] is the most important decision I'll make."

Make Sure Everyone Plays Their Part

Conductors ensure that everyone plays their part, plays it well, and plays in sync. What would happen if the violinist in a chamber quartet was off tempo and off key from the violist? What would have happened if jazz saxophonist John Coltrane hadn't meshed with trumpeter Miles Davis? Luckily, they did mesh well—at least onstage. The situation offstage was more complicated. It isn't a given that musicians will click. Someone, the Conductor, is there to ensure that they do.

Leaders as Conductors are there to do the same thing in the realm of successful businesses. How can a sales team do its job effectively if a supply chain group hasn't arranged for sufficient customer inventory? How can a finance team create a solid pro forma fiscal plan if the sales team hasn't provided an accurate sales forecast? A strong Conductor helps everyone on the team understand both their importance as individual players and the impact they each have on the unity and strength of the Ensemble. To build and strengthen accountability, teach your team members to ask the following three questions of themselves, or a variation on them:

1. What will I do? This zeroes in on the specific action that each individual is going to commit to, without avoiding personal accountability or deflecting or delegating to others.

2 When will I do it? By what date or time will an individual complete this action?

3 How will I let others know? This one question encompasses several others. By what means will I inform other people in my organization that I have completed my task? If there is a delay, how will I let others know about it and what steps will I take to get back on track? Is there a common or preferred method of communicating this information in a collaborative fashion (for example, sharing files on a cloud service or using a project-management tracking hub rather than sending a mass email)?

As you shape your environment, remember that Conductors foster group accountability in an environment where individual team members make their passions and commitments visible to their peers. It's possible to shirk responsibility when one other person is involved, but it's much harder when there's an entire group watching. As for the Conductor, it's incredibly satisfying to witness the whole that emerges from the sum of many parts played well.

I'd like to leave you with a quote that is commonly attributed to Blaine Lee, the vice president of Covey Leadership Center: "The great leaders are like the best conductors—they reach beyond the notes to reach the magic in the players." Indeed, I'd say great Conductors are among the best leaders.

MAKE YOUR DEMO

Once again, reach for your Maestro Mode listening skills—specifically, mode 4. What do you notice is needed in terms of Conducting? Using the tools outlined in this chapter, how can you add leadership impact in terms of bringing a vision to life? How can you bring people together to achieve a common goal and create a safe and productive space for them to perform in harmony?

6

THE PERFORMER

Maximize Your Dynamic Range

"The music is not in the notes, but in the silence between."
WOLFGANG AMADEUS MOZART

THE STAGE goes dark at a Chicago venue in the spring of 1978 where an unknown band is opening for the legendary Journey. After a short drum fill introduction, a spotlight shines on the center of the stage and the immense sound of an electric guitar unlike anything the crowd has ever heard before explodes from the amplifiers on the stage. In the spotlight is a young guitar player from Pasadena, California. He proceeds to create a unique sound that ends up reinventing rock guitar playing. His brilliant technique mixed with passion, dazzling speed, and revolutionary sound will become the gold standard by which all rock guitar performance will be judged from then on. That young performer is Edward Van Halen, and he will be considered godlike to young guitarists and rock music fans for generations to come. In music, as in business, performance is the end goal. It is what is measured, evaluated, and deemed a success or failure. The critics come out to see a performance and write up a review. This is likely familiar territory, regardless of your background. So what is the role of the Performer in the Ensemble Model? In our leadership model, it's the Composer who establishes the vision and the Conductor who creates a space where their team members and leaders can succeed. The role of the Performer is to translate and transform the Composer's vision into reality.

This transformation is a four-part exercise that begins with *comprehension*. A Performer takes the Composer's instructions and seeks to understand those fully before beginning to perform. Then comes *interpretation*; once familiar with the task at hand, the Performer interprets the directions, drawing upon their own skills, experience, and knowledge to do so. The result is also influenced by a mix of curiosity, artistry, and *inspiration*, one reason why no two performances are the same. The last part of the exercise is *expression*: a combination of technical mastery, experience, and courage form the work without bending it out of shape.

All leaders know the importance of a great performance—of seeing an ambitious work through from start to finish. Whether you are tasked with completing a high-visibility project, presenting to the board of directors, or pitching to a client, you must bring heart, mind, and dedication to the task so you can perform at your best. Yet organizations often struggle to use and realize their Performers' potential. A thoughtful step that helps Performers lead at their best begins with listening. Top-level leaders as Performers begin, as they do in many musical endeavors, by listening so they can banish assumptions and truly understand what is happening and what is needed to create the best performance.

Listen to Yourself

Above all, as a Performer, you must listen to yourself. Prompt your listening with these two questions: What's my intention? And what do I want to accomplish?

Your answers will hinge on listening to yourself in relation to the other members of your Ensemble. For example, when you are presented with a task, you may have a strong desire to hit the ground running and rush quickly into action. You might be too eager to do what's been asked of you—too quick to solve the problem, fix the issue, complete the task. By leaping in like this, you risk destroying the bigger performance, which isn't about one note, or one movement, but about working with others, from start to finish, to accomplish a mission. In his book *The First 90 Days*, Michael D. Watkins speaks magnificently to this trap that he calls a "bias to action."

Many of us encounter leadership challenges that result not from a dearth of skill but rather from a lack of reflection on our intentions. Instead of focusing on what you need to do or accomplish, take time to dwell on who you are as a leader. That focus on *being* will attune you to how you prepare and show up for a task. As the saying goes, 80 percent of success is showing up.

If you want to remedy this leap-into-action impulse, it helps to think about how musicians weigh intention and outcome and about how they study a script before they begin. In this way, you can learn to begin a task with the right mindset. Just as a cellist can conjure a sense of *maestoso*, or majesty, in their performance, a leader as Performer can bring similar majesty—or passion, creativity, or accountability—to the next team meeting.

Not long ago I was coaching a woman who was anxious about an upcoming interview for a new role. She was also a musician in her nonwork life and had recently given a performance of which she was particularly proud. When I asked what had allowed her to perform so well, her reply was definitive: "I brought an intention for calm into the performance."

"So how will you bring *that* into the interview?" I asked, and she immediately knew the answer, having already demonstrated the ability to summon calmness. No surprise, then, that she landed the role. Other would-be Performers may have arrived prepared to answer questions, but my client telegraphed the kind of focus, clarity, and intent that employers strive to find.

Listen to the Audience

The job of an audience at a concert is to listen to the show. One job of a Performer, onstage or off, is to listen to the audience. And you can, too, in a business setting. Using your eyes to process body language, ears to hear claps or cheers (or yawns), and intuition to judge less overt reactions, you can gain valuable insights. The next time you're in a meeting, try doing just this. Is the person next to you crossing their arms and sitting back from the table or smiling and leaning in towards you? Are others in the room silent or making encouraging comments? Does the room feel awkward and uncomfortable or alive with possibility and opportunity? Master Performers recognize all of these cues as they employ a powerful concept called maximizing dynamic range.

In music, *dynamic range* refers to how well a recording or live show accommodates a wide range of sound. Percussionists embody this concept profoundly. They might make subtle, magical strikes on a triangle or turn the timpani into a cauldron of rolling thunder. Either way, they move listeners to the extent that is called for by the music in that time and place.

Any idea that all instruments should be played at equal volume and with the same frequency is, of course, preposterous, and its implementation would make for a chaotic concert. Yet in the working world, it's amazing how many teams fail to maximize their Performers' dynamic range and how many leaders fail to properly guide Performers in this respect. Imagine walking into a meeting where the presenter speaks at the same volume and speed, and with the same tone, for half an hour. It would be unbearable. In my estimation, that speaker would need top-to-bottom skills training and coaching.

To maximize dynamic range, you need to build the right skill sets and pick up the right tools. In other words, a brilliant performance requires knowing how to play and what to play.

Learn to Play Dynamically

In his must-read book *What Got You Here Won't Get You There*, leadership expert and executive coach Marshall Goldsmith centers his focus on the fact that the very skills that serve us well early in our career, namely analytical and technical skills, cannot propel us as we progress in our journey because soft skills such as listening and decision-making become more important.

One veteran journalist related to me how, over the course of several decades, he saw many reporters at his major metropolitan daily promoted to leadership positions after accomplishing something big, such as winning a Pulitzer Prize. But many of those reporters failed—in some cases spectacularly—because the skills that made them great journalists had little or nothing to do with how well they could motivate teams or guide people. As he saw it, many were ill-suited to the task because they were introverted and accustomed to working alone and so lacked basic people skills. Their defective leadership style was a default one of mixed messages conveyed as "you'll figure it out" and "because I said so." As Goldsmith puts it, often when someone says "you'll figure it out," they do so with the intention of letting people think for themselves, but those people likely perceive the statement as indicating they've been ignored. Meanwhile, when leaning on a phrase like "because I said so," though the speaker thinks they have all the answers, others perceive such a statement as arrogance.

When you cannot see what others see, or hear what they hear, you miss crucial cues. You lead as though in a world of your own when what you need is to do is *broaden your dynamic range*. Goldsmith argues that you must learn to expand your leadership skill set—or, as I say, learn how to play. People who struggle with broadening their skill sets lean on a narrow set of skills that they mastered earlier in their career but often don't apply later.

In 1941, Ted Williams became a baseball legend after hitting over .400 in a season, the last player to do so. But he also became legendary for being a lousy manager. Meanwhile, mediocre players such as Earl Weaver of the Baltimore Orioles, Sparky Anderson of the Cincinnati Reds, and Joe Maddon of the Chicago Cubs turned into championship managers who brought home World Series trophies. Why? Weaver, Anderson, and Maddon all expanded their dynamic range by leveraging new and different skills for greater impact.

Master musicians understand this principle implicitly, and many have a drive to grow their skills. Right up until his death at age eighty, jazz drummer Jerry Granelli (who backed pianist Vince Guaraldi on the Peanuts soundtracks, including *A Charlie Brown Christmas*) maintained a regular practice regimen where he worked on riffs and techniques to increase his skills. It's worth noting that he also reinforced his learnings by teaching and mentoring a full slate of students. Granelli once reflected on the secret to playing at a high level, saying, "What does it take to play music with another human being? Very interestingly enough, what it takes is the same things to live together as human beings."

On the stage, Performers work in real time to adjust four levers: pitch, tempo, dynamics, and timbre. Their ability to move all four at once does not equate to multitasking, which in many business settings stands in as a shallow substitute for high performance. Rather, these levers work as part of an integrated whole.

Pitch

Jazz trumpeter Wynton Marsalis works pitch in a number of ways, whether by playing high to stir passion or lower notes to express more reflectiveness. How might a leader in a professional setting leverage pitch? Consider a town hall presentation in which you, as a presenter, can literally and figuratively adjust your pitch throughout to create an emotive arc. And, yes, a presentation is often a performance, as the late Steve Jobs well understood when preparing to unveil new Apple products.

If you start in low register ("We are facing competitive headwinds"), you can then move up to medium ("We need everyone's commitment"), and finish in a higher pitch ("Let's make it happen; we have unlimited potential ahead"). Successful TED Talk speakers demonstrate this performance style time and again. Look up TED Talks by the late arts education expert Sir Ken Robinson, social psychologist Amy Cuddy, or communications expert Julian Treasure, whose talk was, appropriately enough, about how to speak so that people will want to listen. You won't hear a single uninspired delivery. Rather, the speakers adjust their pitch throughout to keep their listeners engaged.

Tempo

This is all about speed. In music, tempo instructions are usually written in Italian, so *lento* means slow and *allegro* denotes fast. Master Performers manage their tempo throughout a performance to ensure they make a continuous and positive impact on the audience. You probably know leaders who work at extremes, either in a constant rush where everything is a fire drill or in a state of nonurgency and procrastination. Good Performers adjust their tempo to the task at hand, be it a weekly staff meeting or a two-year strategic project. They may start *lento*, ramp up to *moderato* (medium), and finish at *allegrissimo* (very fast).

I learned a lesson in tempo when I composed, performed, and recorded an album of original music. (It's called *Daydream*, by the way. Look it up!) I was surprised and amused when I realized that many of my initial performances clocked in at exactly eighty beats per minute. My Grammy-nominated producer, Liam Davis, pointed out that this lack of variety compromised the listener's experience because everything I played ended up sounding the same. When I adjusted the tempo at which I played, I produced a far livelier, more dynamic set of songs. (I'll share more about Liam in the next chapter about the Producer.)

Dynamics

Dynamics is a word used to describe levels of volume. The formal name for a piano is *pianoforte*, so named because it's capable of playing volumes ranging from *piano* (soft) to *forte* (loud). Top-rank musical performers take advantage of both of those levels, as well as of volumes in between and beyond, including *mezzo forte* (moderately loud) and *fortissimo* (very loud). They also employ *crescendos*, transitions from soft to loud, and *decrescendos*, which move in the opposite direction. This is how musicians use dynamics to keep an audience engaged. Leader Performers similarly adjust their dynamics for maximum impact. You can employ one volume for one-on-one meetings and another for client conferences or strategic planning sessions.

Now, think about those TED Talk speakers I mentioned earlier, as well as about great orators such as Winston Churchill and Martin Luther King Jr. In every case, you'll see they employed volume dynamics. Even if you can't remember a thing that was said, you will recall how they said it. So use dynamics intentionally. Great musicians and leaders decide when to speak softly, and they decide when to crescendo and bring an audience to its feet.

Timbre

The principal oboist in an orchestra is chosen not only for their technical mastery and accuracy but also their timbre, or tone, which refers to the sound quality they make with their instrument. We all react to tone—for example, you may have heard someone say, "Please don't use that tone with me." Tone can be situational but also personal and something musicians work on over the course of their lifetime. Edward Van Halen spoke often of searching for his ideal tone, something he called his "brown sound."

The best leaders make it a point to use timbre to their advantage, but some leaders aren't aware of the impact made by the resonance of their voice. For example, some may provide colleagues with feedback in a strident tone that indicates little-to-no positive reinforcement, or at other times they might speak in a monotone that betrays a lack of interest in their team members. Goldsmith points to a frequent lack of 360-degree feedback surveys as a reason why so many leaders fumble. They're unaware of their tone and are either unwilling or too distracted to take cues from the audience and players they would otherwise inspire.

We would all rather be leaders who inspire their team members and make them feel valuable and capable. To do this you need to speak with a warm tone. And a warm tone, incidentally, is also helpful for attracting, hiring, and retaining employees. In the current war for talent, many companies have adopted jargon and acronyms worthy of battlefield logistics—think of "skill sets," "KPIs," and "core competencies." When you add this to the growing trend of résumé screening via artificial intelligence—and even though these tools and talking points might have a place in hiring and elsewhere—the lack of warm tone often leaves employees feeling displaced. It may even encourage people to search for a different opportunity, especially if they perceive you to be just another tone-deaf boss. By contrast, those same people will often stick with you and your organization when your tone is inviting and inspirational.

This is part of what makes tone, or timbre, so crucial: you either draw people in or you lose them after the opening notes. So work on your tone and take cues from those around you. And remember that pure tone takes many musicians a lifetime to achieve.

Leadership is performance in every sense of the word. And though you often don't have a choice of *when* you must perform, you can always choose *how*. Even when you are asked to improvise, you can always step up with intent. That I've used the word *intention* several times so far in this chapter is no accident. Great improv performers don't wing things entirely, and neither do great leaders. No matter the stage, Performers reflect on what they're trying to achieve and its desired effect before sounding the very first note.

Choose Your Leadership Instrument

As Performers, one of the most important things you can do to serve the composition is to choose your instrument wisely. Leadership is contextual, as different situations call for different styles of leadership. The same is true of music and instruments. When playing pop or jazz, I might reach for my 1993 Fender Custom Shop Stratocaster due to its rich and bright, clean tone. For a hard rock performance, though, I may need to bring my 2022 Les Paul Custom, which provides a deep, warm tone.

As a Performer, you always need to leverage the High Fidelity Listening Methodology discussed in chapter 2 and listen for what is needed by the audience, your fellow Ensemble members, and the composition. Use what you hear in order to select the appropriate instrument. For Performers who are leading in professional contexts, the process is the same. You must listen to your audience (which might include customers, partners, vendors, or even competitors) and to your fellow Ensemble members, and you must consider the composition you intend to perform. Does your project have a moderate tempo requiring a bright tone with a few long, sustained notes—or is it fast right from the start? As the advice goes, always bring the right tool (instrument!) for the job, a truism that holds whether you're building a house, performing Beethoven's *Fifth*, or leading a corporate turnaround.

In the leadership realm, the classic context for bringing the right (or wrong) instrument to the job often happens in the process of delivering and soliciting feedback. I'll delve into this topic in greater detail in the next chapter about the leader as Producer, but here are a couple of examples to illustrate how a leader's tone and tempo made all the difference.

When I was pursuing my MBA, I interned with a firm known for their extensive focus on leadership development training. I was assigned a challenging project for the summer with little direction from my manager, who made it clear he had no time for me. After weeks of work, I submitted my presentation and eagerly awaited his feedback. Several days later, he summoned me into his office and said bluntly, "Stephen, one needs either credible data or credibility and you have neither." He handed my presentation back to me and said flatly, "Begin again." Did I mention that these were the most words he had spoken to me so far that summer? Wham! I felt completely demoralized. Later on, I would realize that though what he said was true, the tone of his message was crushing.

Years later I was working in a different organization and was responsible for creating a high-visibility strategic plan to help grow a new division. I took my presentation to the

CMO. As I was new to the organization, I was nervous about the feedback. Instead, the CMO started with "I really love what you've done here... I'd love to brainstorm with you a bit." What proceeded was a brilliant case study in feedback delivery. He led with highlighting specific examples of what he liked and thought were impactful strategies. He then embodied leadership curiosity by asking me about some key areas. After I explained my rationale, I contributed further questions using phrases such as "I wonder...," "How might we...," and "What if..." As he provided constructive critiques in response, they never felt personal. And then he ended our conversation with the master stroke: "How can I support you?" I left feeling energized, engaged, and ready to drive the new strategy on behalf of the organization.

Finally, I'd like to leave you with a cautionary tale about dynamic range, one that highlights the importance of not just having it but exercising judgment about how to use it.

As referenced at the beginning of this book, some of the first leadership lessons I learned came from my high school rock band, Onyx. After our exciting Battle of the Bands performance, we had been hired to play another gig the next day: a six-year-old's birthday party. As we all know, there's a world of difference between high school headbangers and elementary school kids barely weaned off Thomas the Tank Engine, but that didn't faze us. In our minds, still basking in the prior night's glory, we were rock stars! And that's why we played the exact same set that we did the evening before. Two songs into our set, a parent told us that children were crying due to our "loud racket," and then she paid us to stop playing.

This story always makes me laugh because it's a failure of listening on many levels. What parent hires a high school rock band for a children's party? Know your audience! But also, what band hired for a children's party shows up and plays "Stairway to Heaven"? It's important to have dynamic range, but it's just as important to exercise it thoughtfully. When it's your colleague's birthday, sing "Happy Birthday" in the conference room. Save the Smashing Pumpkins' "Ava Adore" for a different time and place.

MAKE YOUR DEMO

Consider rehearsing with one or more of these leader-as-performer experiments.

- Before your next meeting or presentation, experiment with altering your emotional and vocal pitch throughout. Now, give your performance a test run, and take note of the impact you have on your audience.

- Adjust your tempo in your next leadership performance and see what happens. In rallying your ensemble, you'll find life beyond eighty beats per minute!

- Adjust your dynamics in your next presentation or meeting. As you discover what works well by experimenting with pitch, tempo, and dynamics, adjust again and repeat.

- Ask yourself, "What is my natural tone?" Is it direct, polite, and upbeat? Or is it glass-half-empty or monotone? If you're brave enough, record yourself and then listen to the recording. Seek feedback from audience members with the best seats in the house: your spouse, trusted colleagues, a best friend, a career coach, counselor, or mentor. Experiment with adjusting your tone to work in some brighter or more striking colors. What do you notice?

7

THE PRODUCER

Bring Out the Best in Others

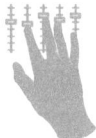

"Make the music sound as good as possible."
DAVID GUETTA

TO SAY RICK RUBIN is a Grammy-winning producer is accurate and yet also incomplete. This is the man who launched Def Jam Recordings with Russell Simmons from his dorm room at New York University and signed a teenaged LL Cool J. Rapper Chuck D told Anderson Cooper on *60 Minutes* that "Rick Rubin is one of the pillar stones of hip-hop," which is impressive enough except that Rubin has worked with artists in many other genres too. He's the person who revived the career of Johnny Cash, convincing the aging country star to cover the Nine Inch Nails song "Hurt." Fascinatingly, Rick Rubin doesn't sing or play a single musical instrument. Yet he is legendary for helping others bring the very best out of their own instruments and compositions.

It was 2002, and Cash had continually refused Rubin's request until the producer patiently coached him into seeing the deeper meaning of the song and how it related to his own rebellious, often tortured spirit. Ultimately, Cash's version of the song, and the video that accompanied it, proved so powerful that songwriter Trent Reznor (who told the British tabloid the *Sun* that hearing the cover initially felt invasive, "like someone kissing your girlfriend") conceded that the Man in Black, as Cash was sometimes called, had captured the spirit of the song.

"I don't even know what a traditional producer is or does. I feel like the job is like being a coach, building good work habits, and building trust," Rubin told the *Washington Post* in 2006. The next year, *Time* magazine named Rubin to its list of the hundred most influential people in the world.

Rubin's methods and values are attainable even for those of us not in the music business, and they point to why the Producer is the fourth member of our leadership Ensemble. So far, I've explored when and why leaders must be Composer, Conductor, and Performer. Now let's add Producer to this list, which requires understanding, perhaps more than Rubin does (or admits he does), exactly what's involved.

What Is a Producer?

George Martin produced the Beatles, Ted Templeman produced Van Halen, and Quincy Jones produced Michael Jackson. Without Martin, there would be no string quartet in the song "Eleanor Rigby." Jones arranged the rhythm section that propelled "Billie Jean." And Templeman convinced

Van Halen to record the groundbreaking track "Eruption" after hearing the guitarist play it as a warm-up exercise. Their contributions were invaluable.

But what exactly does a music producer do? It's a question that's surprisingly hard to answer. Few industry experts can agree on a single definition, but there seems to be one constant: the goal of a producer is always to "make the music sound as good as possible," or so goes a quotation attributed to the French deejay and producer David Guetta, who has worked with artists including the Black Eyed Peas, Kelly Rowland, and Kelis. The job of producer encompasses a number of dimensions, from composition and arrangement to guiding artists to realize their vision.

How does producing apply to the world of leadership? Simply put, Producers foster excellence in their charges by turning ideas and inspiration into tangible results. Theirs is an example you can, and should, strive to follow.

First and foremost, Producers need to bring out the best in others. In his seminal 1970 extended essay *The Servant as Leader*, Robert K. Greenleaf coined the titular term that defines a best-practice leadership philosophy. The servant-leader puts others first. For us, "others" means everyone whose lives we touch, including direct reports, peers, customers, vendors, and the people cleaning your office at night. Putting others first helps us to recognize the talent that is in front of our eyes and others may miss. This is how Martin saw promise in Geoff Emerick, an unproven twenty-year-old kid, and made him the engineer on the Beatles' *Revolver* album, which included "Eleanor Rigby." Emerick went on to win four Grammy awards.

Producer Jack Antonoff brought out the best in Taylor Swift on her chart-busting *Midnights* album by putting Swift's vision and music first, not his own. At the same time, he delineated the path for Swift to move from vision to achievement. The best Producers do the same for people around them. Rather than prescribe or dictate via obsolete and obstinate models of leadership (the "because I said so" way of doing things), primo Producers listen. They remain curious. They support.

Musical tracks get off to a great start when the drummer or another band member counts in—you can sometimes catch someone saying "One, two, three, four" before the music starts. In the same way, leadership Producers have their own four count, which goes like this.

One: Clarify the Goal

The best producers and leaders start by asking deep questions focused on realizing others' goals. These questions run the gamut from the overarching—"What do you really want?"—to the specific—"What exactly does success look like?" My personal favorite, and one that I've embraced in my own leadership journey, is this: "What would an absolutely inspiring outcome be?" Note that these questions focus on the other person. They aren't about what the Producer wants or thinks should be done.

In 2022 I released an album, *Daydream*, which benefited mightily from having a fantastic producer, Liam Davis. In leadership terms, he functioned like a coach, bringing out the best in terms of my songwriting and performance. He asked me, "How would you describe your vision for the album?" That got me thinking, and my answers formed the architecture I used to build the collection of songs.

I also realized that the best managers in my corporate career all asked a variation of the same question, wanting to know my goal and how they could support me in achieving it.

Let's say a team is paralyzed by a plethora of choices and questions. The best Producers provide guardrails, limit distractions, and help others identify what they *don't* want. They may ask, "What values are nonnegotiable for you?" and "What will you not tolerate?" These questions can illuminate paths to reaching worthwhile goals. In a recent coaching session with a client who struggled over whether to take a lucrative job offer, I asked her what she would no longer tolerate. "A long commute," she responded. The prospective job required a long commute. She said no to the offer, and not long after that she found a fabulous job with the short commute that she wanted.

Just as smart paths require sure steps, Producers and their Performers need a plan of action to realize the vision they've defined. Nile Rodgers, a producer as well as cofounder of the disco band Chic, helps his artists construct a track list and even a release date for an album. In much the same way, the best Producers might encourage their direct reports to create plans with structure. This can seem overwhelming, but when plans are broken down from annual ones into quarterly, monthly, and weekly tasks, clarity emerges. In my many years in new product development, I worked on lots of "road maps," visual plans that identify a series of key milestones to reach over a period of time. I always found them to be useful.

Two: Create Accountability

After a Producer has helped an individual clarify what they do and don't want, and how they plan to accomplish that, it's time to commit. Producers work to keep an artist focused and inspired, which isn't easy if an artist has to sing the same passage hundreds of times in the studio. In a memorable scene from the Ritchie Valens biopic *La Bamba*, actor Lou Diamond

Phillips delivers the opening lines of "Come On, Let's Go" over and over and over, showing the arduous path to creating an indelible hit.

Producers make for potent accountability partners, as they're tasked with reminding the other person *what* they committed to, *why* it is important, *how* they should take the next necessary step, and *when* they need to complete that step or the overall project.

As a coach, I like to use a technique where clients self-define how they want to be held accountable and also agree to a consequence they'll suffer if they fall short. The consequences are often funny. Failure might mean eating their least favorite vegetable for a week, giving money to a political party that they detest, or listening to their least favorite style of music. (By the way, why do so many people dislike disco? It has some amazing qualities!)

Three: Solicit and Provide Feedback

In the same way that veteran producer Jim Abbiss helped a young Adele find power and nuance in her voice, the best Producers provide valuable feedback to their Performers. Imagine a young Adele singing "Rolling in the Deep" or "Rumour Has It" by herself and without guidance. It's hard to imagine that she would have ended up with the songs that we now know so well and that went on, as part of the album *21*, to sell more than thirty-one million copies.

Despite the countless leadership articles on the importance of soliciting and delivering feedback, many leaders still struggle to do it. Giving and getting feedback can be uncomfortable and awkward, a major reason many supervisors resist 360-degree feedback surveys that could improve their performance. But there are some ways to deliver feedback effectively, starting with the classic SBI method:

- **Situation:** Provide a situation that connects the context to the feedback ("John, in yesterday's team meeting...").
- **Behavior:** Indicate the behavior where you want to provide feedback ("I noticed that when you replied to your colleague's question...").
- **Impact:** Articulate how the behavior had an impact on others or the situation ("everybody in the room became very uncomfortable").

Then there's my favorite method, the "even better if" / "I wonder" approach, which my vocal coach Jess Godwin used with me. I love how it affirms while setting a higher target. "I really liked that last try. Nice breath support and tone—very warm," she told me when I was preparing my voice for an upcoming gig. "Now, I wonder what would happen if you added a bit more emotion to it. Let's try that and see what happens." Note that she balanced what I'd done well with where I could improve, while also introducing an element of experimentation.

The best Producers provide bracing, honest, and supportive feedback. But they also see that feedback is a two-way street. Producers at the elite level routinely ask artists how they want to be produced—not to coddle them, but to get the best out of them. Gone are the days, at least in any workplace that wants to be considered progressive, when feedback flowed downhill from manager to direct report. Ideally, feedback branches out in all directions and is offered also to managers, peers, direct reports, customers, and vendors. You should solicit feedback even as you deliver it to others. My most inspiring managers over the years have asked, "What's one thing I can work on to be a better leader?"

Four: Listen for Possibility

The best Producers are constantly listening—and not, as discussed in chapter 2, listening with the intent to respond (LITR). Instead, they're listening for what might be possible, listening for opportunity. Music producers listen to the artist, then to the music, and then to the intended audience to anticipate its response. Anticipating the audience's reaction might sound like a form of pandering, but this can be how crossover hits and artists are made. Producers know and honor their audiences by listening for their feedback and input.

When Brian Wilson produced the now-classic song "God Only Knows," he worked closely with accomplished studio musicians to flesh out the ideas he heard from them. He didn't merely dictate how the musicians should play; he sought their input. As I mentioned in chapter 5, he had his ensemble play instruments that were nontraditional for rock, including French horns, sleigh bells, clarinets, harpsicord, and even orange plastic cups. In the mid-1960s, this was revolutionary, and Wilson was just twenty-four years old at the time. He made an already strong composition even stronger. Listening proved key in his success.

Similarly, the best Producers listen for possibility, which can mean listening for ways to help their company innovate, support a high-potential employee's career path, or streamline a process in need of an update.

Producers should also ask "What if?" In 1985, Russell Simmons asked, "What if we combined rap and rock?" For his production of "Walk This Way," an Aerosmith cover, he teamed the Boston hard rock band with New York hip-hop pioneers Run-DMC. The result was a genre-bending foray into something not heard before.

Steve Jobs of Apple asked "What if?" when he combined email, web search, a music player, and a phone to produce the world's first iPhone. Bill Gates of Microsoft did the same when he turned computers from examples of primitive green-screen technology into portals for programs that were intuitive to use for internet searches, writing, and more.

The Producer as General Manager

Some music producers, especially of electronic music, don't play an instrument. When Rick Rubin was showing Anderson Cooper around his home studio, Shangri-La, he said he could barely play music or work a soundboard. Still, producers usually possess a mix of technical, artistic, and people skills. Rubin claimed to have no technical skills, but he clearly knew others who did and worked with them, as well as with artists, managers, and others in his orbit. One day in a music producer's life might be spent helping the Foo Fighters tap their inner muse, and the next might involve finalizing release schedules, booking studio time, and hiring session musicians.

The most effective Producers are versatile. They think analytically, grasp the human side of leadership, and know the importance of creating "followership" throughout their organizations. If you have a strong aptitude for the technical, ask yourself how you might expand your understanding of how to motivate people. If you have the intuitive nature of an artist, think about ways you can add structure to freely flowing ideas. The most effective Producers blend it all.

In his work with the Beatles, Martin knew how to arrange strings, find exotic instruments, and communicate ideas to his recording engineers. He coaxed great performances out of the band, a classic example being that he pushed John Lennon to give "Twist and Shout" a try in the studio on a day that Lennon's voice was shot after a full day's singing. The result was arguably the best cover song the Beatles ever recorded. (The song was originally recorded by the R&B group the Top Notes, and then the Isley Brothers.) On the track "In My Life," Martin played a baroque piano solo that was recorded at half speed and an octave lower so that it ended up sounding almost like a harpsichord. It was Martin who masterminded and executed Lennon's wish to combine two session tracks recorded in different keys and speed into the stunning sonic journey of "Strawberry Fields Forever."

Unsurpassed leaders are Producers who, with time, patience, and practice, give life to hits. They don't mind saving the spotlight for their Performers either. In fact, that is how they galvanize the kind of partnerships that outperform, outshine, and outlast all others. As Rubin did, they coach, build, work, and foster trust.

MAKE YOUR DEMO

Call up your mode 4, Maestro Mode, listening skills again (chapter 2). What do you notice is needed in terms of Producing? Who might benefit from support to bring out their best for a performance? How might you help them lean into their superpowers to make a massive impact?

8

THE FAN

Follow, Celebrate, Support

"What we create doesn't live on unless there's an audience to remember it."

LADY GAGA

B Y NOW you've learned why music is the perfect lens for leadership, how to take the first step towards effective leadership, and why every single step on the journey has to involve listening. I've introduced you to the Audira Ensemble Model and four of its leadership roles: Composer, Conductor, Performer, and Producer. You've learned about each role individually and some tips for working with them. When you master all four roles, and especially if you can do so well enough to teach them to others, you're most of the way to leading a dynamic, exciting, creative Ensemble.

And yet what's an ensemble without an audience? That's especially true for a group that has rehearsed and prepared for a performance and is fired up to fill a space with sound. Every professional musician I've ever met is in the business because they love music and, in some cases, can't imagine doing anything else, but they also want to share it. There is nothing quite so lonely as an empty concert hall on a night it should be filled. This leads me to the fifth member of our Ensemble, whose presence drives the rest: the Fan.

It can be hard, at first, to understand why a Fan is a leader on par with the others in our Ensemble. After all, when Rihanna takes the stage in front of thousands, does every member of her audience have responsibility equivalent to her own? No, of course not. But in the Ensemble Model, a Fan is not one person in the bleachers but a specific person others depend on for encouragement. The Producer elicits the best from a Performer, but the Fan inspires the Composer, Conductor, Performer, and Producer too. A Fan might be the best friend at a wedding, a supportive customer at work, an influential mentor, or a neighbor applauding your volunteer efforts. The Fan plays a supportive role but not a supporting one. If the Fan weren't around, the Ensemble might still play, but its performance and tour would likely sound very different.

Some of the greatest musicians describe themselves first and foremost as fans. In chapter 2 I mentioned that the Foo Fighters' Dave Grohl had a life-changing moment as an audience member at a Naked Raygun concert. He was a Fan that night and many other nights too. In a 1997 interview with *Guitar World*, Grohl talked about Kurt Cobain, who was both his bandmate in Nirvana and, for a time, his roommate in a tiny apartment. "For the longest time, we didn't have a television.

We didn't have anything to do. So we'd spend these gray Olympia, Washington, afternoons just playing guitars and messing around with a 4-track, or working on harmonies," said Grohl. "Through Kurt, I saw the beauty of minimalism and the importance of music that's stripped down." Those are the words of a roomie, an Ensemble partner, and an admiring Fan.

Elvis Presley provided another example of fandom. At a 1969 press conference in Las Vegas, a journalist referred to him as "the king." "No, *that's* the real King of Rock 'n' Roll," said Elvis, gesturing to his hero Fats Domino, who was in the room. Freddie Mercury, of Queen, was a fan as well: "Led Zeppelin is the greatest. Robert Plant is one of the most original vocalists of our time. As a rock band they deserve the kind of success they're getting," he told *Circus Magazine* in 1975. And John Lennon, for his part, gushed on a talk show in 1972 about one of his favorite musicians: "If you tried to give rock and roll another name, you might call it Chuck Berry." In an interview with *DigBoston*, legendary multi-instrumentalist and composer Cory Wong referenced how seeing his idol, Victor Wooten (jazz bass player extraordinaire, part of Béla Fleck and the Flecktones), gave him this realization: "I was asking myself, 'Do I have permission to do this?' And after seeing the Flecktones live it was a resounding 'Yes, you're allowed to do whatever you want if it's compelling.'"

Many if not most musicians got their start, and discovered their love of music, as fans—and continue to play the Fan role all of their lives. I'm especially fond of the story about Edward Van Halen attending a Tool concert in Los Angeles with his son. A concertgoer posing in front of the stage asked Edward to take a photo, thinking he was just another Tool fan—which he was, in addition to being one of the world's greatest guitarists. (Van Halen's son, Wolfgang, took a photo of his dad fulfilling the request and posted it online, where it went viral.) In another viral photo, Dave Grohl was captured screaming his head off in the front row of a Metallica concert at the Rose Bowl. He was just a normal, paying audience member loving the experience, like everyone else. That said, the photo was posted online under the headline "Dave Grohl Goes to Metallica Concert like an Ordinary Dude" in an article that also quotes Grohl as saying, "I'll be a die-hard Metallica fan until the day I die."

This look of admiration is not one that has historically resonated in corporate America. General Electric CEO Jack Welch, recently called "the first celebrity CEO," reveled in bowing to no one and being feared by all. But the post-Welch years revealed fatal flaws in his approach, and today's GE is a shell of its former self due in large part to vulnerabilities he created for his successors. The twenty-first century calls for a different leadership style, one involving humility.

Pivoting between Leader and Follower

When I was applying to business school, I was taught a vivid lesson highlighting the importance of followership as a form of leadership. As part of the application process, I was required to participate in an in-person interview with the admissions team. After smoothly answering the interviewer's initial questions on how I had led in a traditional sense, I was stopped cold in my tracks by a far better question: "And give us some examples of when you led by following?" (Not surprisingly, after providing a fairly weak answer, I was not accepted into that particular school.) Our society still places significant emphasis on the performers taking the stage, and people with aspirations to lead may be reluctant to take on the role of Fan. In response to this, I would like to make several points. First, hierarchical organizations often imply a rigid demarcation of responsibilities, but in the Ensemble Model roles are fluid. Becoming a Fan does not mean remaining in that role, and only that role, forever.

Second, without Fans, the people onstage are bereft of purpose. If you have ever witnessed a stadium full of concertgoers singing the tag of "Hey Jude" while Paul McCartney and his bandmates step back, then you likely know this. Leaders—whether they are Composers, Conductors, Performers, or Producers—not only know how to elevate Fans but also consider themselves part of a larger ecosystem.

Third, the very premise of the Ensemble Model is listening, a behavior closely associated with following. To lead, you have to be able to set aside your ego, listen to the dynamics of a group, and identify what is needed. Perhaps you've been to a meeting where all the type A personalities tried to control the agenda. If you've sat through an experience like this, you know how frustrating it is for everyone else and how much it impedes productive group dynamics. If there's a need on a team for someone to follow, don't be afraid to do just that.

In the Ensemble Model, leader and follower are not polar opposites as they are on the typical leadership continuum. There must be balance, and the role of the leader as Fan helps maintain that balance. As I've telegraphed throughout this book, the best leaders begin by asking two questions, or variations of them, to ground themselves: "What does this task, objective, or goal need?" and "What is my ideal role to support this?" And then they take the time to listen to their internal answers and dig deeper as needed.

The role of Fan showcases an important trait: patience. In chapter 1 I talked about how intention is a core principle of leadership. Anyone can lead if they embody three core elements: intent, action, and impact. That said, if you have strong intent, you may dive directly into action. You may default to jumping into any challenge immediately and declaring yourself the person in charge. But what if you're not the person best suited for that role at that particular time? Sometimes the right role to play in such a moment is that of a Fan.

The humility involved in being a Fan can pay dividends and lead to remarkable results. Steven Spielberg (creator of *Jaws*, *E.T. the Extra Terrestrial*, *Jurassic Park*, *Schindler's List*, and so many more) ranks as one of the greatest living film directors. But at the same time, he is a Fan of George Lucas (of *Star Wars* franchise fame), and the two worked together on the *Indiana Jones* films. Throughout his career, Spielberg has turned to Lucas to provide the special effects in his movies rather than take on that task himself. By asking Lucas to join him, Spielberg was in a sense Conducting and putting "the right people in the right chairs at the right time," as I wrote about in chapter 5. But I'm pretty sure that George Lucas doesn't say yes to just anyone who comes his way. Spielberg, as a Fan, had authenticity and credibility in making the ask. A Fan creates, respects, and builds upon relationships.

Asking someone else to take over a task can benefit the entire Ensemble. Several years ago, shortly after founding Audira, I was part of a leadership development retreat program that involved attending a series of four weeklong sessions, over the course of a year, in the mountains of North Carolina. Participants engaged in team-building activities that were often outdoors and required collaboration, communication, and—this is key—identifying who would lead and who would follow.

During one of our final activities, which involved ropes, a ball, and a knowledge of physics, I was designated the group leader. But it didn't take me long to realize that my lack of physics knowledge posed a problem and compromised my ability to lead the group to success. I also recognized that we had a ringer in our midst, a natural who could compensate for my deficiency. One of my group members had a physics and engineering background, constructed buildings for a living, and was extremely handy, to put it mildly. I asked him to take over as leader and became a Fan who was treated to quite a performance when our group completed the task faster than any other. My morphing from Conductor to Fan proved to be the best decision for the team.

Many customers of Apple products don't realize that the late Steve Jobs knew little if anything about how to build the company's devices. Apple's cofounder, Steve Wozniak, handled that part. Nor did Jobs know how to design the devices; that was the job of Jony Ive. Jobs, a computer geek and calligraphy student, was a Fan of both men. Had Jobs tried to take the lead on what were ultimately their tasks, iPhones and MacBooks would not exist as they do today. Instead, Jobs took on the roles in which he excelled. As a Composer, he visualized future products. As a Conductor, he put the right people in the right seats. As a Performer, he presented products with great fanfare. (He was known for saying, "One more thing..." at announcements.) As a Producer, he enabled his team members to achieve things they never thought possible—through what Walter Isaacson, in his book *Steve Jobs*, references as the "Reality Distortion Field," an ability to convince himself and others of almost anything. But during product development, Jobs was a Fan who cheered for the team (albeit, in what many describe, to be his own unique "tough love" way).

A Crucial Role in the Ensemble

When you have an opportunity to serve as a Fan for your fellow Performers, embrace that opportunity and ask yourself what they need from you. Sometimes they may need applause and reassurance, while at other times they might need your focus and attention. In the end, leaders succeed when their teams do well. A Fan is very much part of that team.

A now classic and famous musical example of the Fan dynamic at work involved the rock band Kiss, known for not only its music but Kabuki makeup and performances that have involved fire-breathing, pyrotechnics, and other shocking stunts. In the early to mid-1970s, radio deejays ignored Kiss, treating the band as too out-there and cartoonish. In 1975, the detractors included a certain Indiana disc jockey who was surprised to learn that Kiss had some fanatical followers in Terre Haute. One of them, a teenager named Bill Starkey, called and told the deejay that if he didn't play a Kiss song, the "Kiss Army" would descend upon the station.

According to a legend that developed (and encouraged by Kiss's publicity department), when the deejay refused, Starkey made good on his promise, and a large group of the band's followers showed up in Kiss makeup at the station and demanded Kiss airplay. Reality is a little less dramatic: according to the *Tribune-Star* of Terre Haute, Starkey and his friends made T-shirts and wrote letters that a new, competing radio station in town read every night. Amid all the attention, Kiss scheduled a concert in Terre Haute, and more than eleven thousand people showed up, about 15 percent of the population and nearly a thousand more than had turned out for Elvis Presley earlier that year. Kiss was elated, presented Starkey with a plaque, and encouraged his army to grow. In

Terre Haute and many other places, Kiss might have been little known if not for its fans.

One of my favorite examples of leader-as-fan came from my own corporate career. When working for the famous grill manufacturer, Weber-Stephen Products, my manager at that time and dear friend, Chris Stephen, would begin and end every conversation with one simple question: "And how can I support you today?" You see, he didn't view his role in the old-school hierarchical, top-down approach with himself as "boss" and me as "underling." Rather, he was there precisely to make *me* successful. He would always say, "Stephen, I am your biggest fan, and I am here to ensure that you are successful."

I'll leave you with one more incredible example of what a Fan can accomplish. In 2016, it appeared that Brian Johnson, the lead singer of AC/DC, would have to retire. After thirty-plus years, increasing deafness meant he could no longer hear guitars and bass onstage. Johnson told a BBC Radio 6 music program, "You get into your motorcar and you can't tell who's singing the song. It's just this noise... you can't tell if it's Paul McCartney or Mick Jagger." Doctor after doctor told him to give up performing.

But Johnson had a Fan in Stephen Ambrose, an audio expert who invented the in-ear monitors that performers everywhere use today. Ambrose issued an open message to Johnson: "Please don't stop performing; help is on the way." After Johnson reached out to Ambrose, the two worked together to solve the problem, and a circle of caring and curing began. The Fan became the leader; the leader became the Fan. A breakthrough came later when Ambrose was able to take an experimental device the size of a car battery and shrink it so that it could be inserted into an ear canal. The

Ambrose Diaphonic Ear Lens works like a second eardrum, using bone conduction to circumvent lost hearing.

From the start, Ambrose spoke as only a Fan can: "If anyone deserves to benefit from my research, it's Brian, who has been giving incomparable performances for years despite increasing hearing loss," he said after Johnson agreed to an initial meeting. Only in allowing Ambrose to take the lead could Johnson return to recording and the live stage, his hard-rock talent once again shining a light for millions.

MAKE YOUR DEMO

As you reflect on your Ensemble and audience members and leverage your listening skills, consider your answers to the following questions:

- *Who needs me as their Fan today?* Perhaps it's a team member, a customer, a family member, or someone you just met who could clearly use a boost of support.

- *How can I cheer for them?* Although grand gestures are nice, so often the most powerful thing we can do for others is to simply be present, to show up. Maybe it's taking them to dinner in appreciation or cheering for them at a soccer game or a debate tournament. Maybe it's encouraging them when they are elected to the local community nonprofit group. Or maybe it's simply being there for them after a tough day at school or work.

There are no wrong answers here—only the opportunity to help lift someone else, like in a mosh pit at a Soundgarden show.

9
THE TOUR
Listen Closely, and Improvise like a Jazz Pro

> *"It's one thing to spend a long time learning how to play well in the studio, but to do it front of people is what keeps me coming back to touring."*
>
> **NEIL PEART**

AS I'VE ILLUSTRATED throughout this book, music is a perfect lens for learning about leadership. The two worlds are similar and even share some common language. I'm going to repeat something I wrote in chapter 6: In music, as in business, performance is the end goal. It is what is measured, evaluated, and deemed a success or failure.

But now that I've repeated that statement, I'd like to amend it slightly. A band doesn't write songs and rehearse endlessly to play just one performance on a single, transformative night. Rather, the band members prepare to give many concerts. Sometimes they even play those concerts in venues across the city, country, or world. In other words, the band's aim is to take the act on tour. This, too, parallels the world outside of music. When you set an intention, it may be to accomplish a single task on time, but more often you are working towards a goal that requires exhibiting and maintaining a high level of performance over time. So, in retrospect, performance is not the end goal; the goal is a tour.

In the leadership and business world, touring could mean taking a strategic plan for a spin to get feedback from employees, shareholders, customers, and vendors. It could mean taking out a prototype product and having beta testers provide honest feedback, even if it's brutal. It could mean growing a company, both according to accepted financial metrics and in terms of customer satisfaction, employee retention, and operational efficiency.

True leadership is tested when potential gets put into practice. My dear friend and mentor Professor Harry Davis equates leadership to a performance art because it is experiential in nature and requires practice. Just as a musical act may practice for months or years in anticipation of a tour, you as leaders must rehearse the concepts I've shared with you so you can apply them and bring them to life. In doing so, in a sense you take your performance out on the road, so that the ensemble you are seeking to showcase no longer exists only in your minds or as words on the pages of a book about leadership. Only when on tour can you truly judge an Ensemble's success. "Work is love made visible," wrote the Lebanese-American poet and artist Kahlil Gibran—and I'd add "made audible," to stick with the driving metaphor of this book.

But going on the road on tour can be scary, and I want to head off the leadership version of stage fright and performance anxiety. In that spirit, let's acknowledge and address the mental traps that we all experience, which include self-doubt, fear of failure, and negative "What if?" spiraling. When moving leadership from the studio to the live tour, I take four steps to prevent these traps from affecting me.

Apply an Experimentation Mindset

I learned this trick from my days in new product development and as an entrepreneur: treat each new move as an experiment. It's much less scary to think of a prototype as an experiment rather than a final, perfect end product. The perfect, it is said, is the enemy of the good, and this seems to be a sentiment shared by musicians and recognized by leaders in other fields. "Do not fear mistakes? There are none," Miles Davis is supposed to have said. Nelson Mandela put it like this: "I never lose. I either win or learn." The late Steven Schnall, the award-winning CEO-founder of Quontic Bank, called this sentiment "try it on."

To try this mindset on for yourself, start by asking, "What do I want to learn?" Let's say that your goal is to express yourself more confidently in front of others. In that case, set up a series of experiments that allows you to try a more assertive manner when speaking in front of others. Start by speaking "publicly" to a trusted friend, before speaking in front of two or three people, and then eventually to a larger group. After each experiment in this study, ask yourself (without judgment) the following questions:

- What did I learn?
- What worked?
- How will I carry that forward?
- What didn't work?
- How will I adjust for that in my next experiment?

Improvise like the Jazz Greats

Thelonious Monk once said, "The piano ain't got no wrong notes." Jazz is full of happy accidents—along with some weird ones, striking ones, flat ones, and mournful ones. Improvisation is a staple of jazz, a magical manifestation of whatever is going on inside a musician's head. Just as the best jazz artists try new things onstage and with an audience watching, so, too, should we all.

The most effective leaders try something, adjust, and try again—and this is particularly important to do when you're on tour. When meeting new audiences, things can be unpredictable, even more so than usual. You have to be nimble, quick-thinking, and able to recover from disappointments. In his book *The Talent Code*, author Daniel Coyle discusses a method of trying something, backing up, getting past the roadblock, and repeating the trial. He holds that this "deep practice" method produces competencies up to ten times faster than unstructured practice while also building confidence and skills that stick around. As I see it, improvisation involves these three core practices.

Listening

Just as the tenor saxophone player is aware of what the trumpeter is doing, we listen to those around us and respond on the basis of what we hear. In business, that could mean listening for market trends and making moves accordingly or listening for our customers' unmet needs and responding with resonance and thoughtfulness. Or it could mean listening to our employees and their ideas, then harnessing their skills and giving them more and better-targeted leadership responsibilities.

Modulating

Savvy leaders notice changes in the air that affect them—key shifts, if you will. When a trumpet player moves from G to C, the tenor saxophonist adjusts and follows. A drummer finishing their solo with an intentionally faster tempo encourages the other musicians in the group to follow suit.

When you notice a market niche faces a disruption, you likely practice agility and adjust; the high-tech sector refers to this as pivoting and iterating. Many organizations practiced this type of modulation during the Covid pandemic. For example, the audio electronics company Sound Devices leveraged its expertise in plastics and made a rapid pivot in order to create personal protection equipment and face masks. Crises have a way of stimulating companies to achieve great things due to necessity.

Playing on the Power of "Yes, And..."

As you learned in chapter 2, the best leaders have the "yes, and..." mindset. The "yes" acknowledges the value of an idea or an initiative; the "and" opens the door to building on it. Say our trumpet player I mentioned earlier changes keys, and the tenor sax not only adjusts and follows but adds a new melody. The musical moves are multiplying, and the audience and other players are intrigued, listening for what might emerge. One idea can spark others, and no one knows where those will lead. 3M famously created a failed glue that didn't stick very well, but engineer Arthur Fry built on that less than sticky substance to create the Post-it Note. Today 3M possesses more than 32,000 patents globally, according to the innovation consultancy GreyB. I wonder how many of those resulted from "yes, and…" experiments.

Listen for Your Leadership Impact

Do you remember the story I told in chapter 6 about my high school band being asked—indeed, paid—to stop playing at a child's birthday party? The most skilled and adventurous musicians constantly update their setlists and performances for different audiences. Musicians who are the least skilled at adjusting for audience impact end up home sooner that they'd have liked to dissect what went wrong.

To measure the impact of your leadership performance, gather feedback from the audience. Listening for audience impact is just as important outside of the music realm and may help root out problems. A senior leader might listen within an organization for whether their employees are feeling engaged, productive, and inspired—and may discover that a previously high-performing leader seems to have checked out. They might listen for the impact a company is having on its customers—and learn that a longtime customer is less than pleased. By listening for impact on social media, a company's public relations team may learn that the CEO's latest comments, made during a formal press conference, didn't go over well with the public.

In all of these cases, listening for impact should inform the leader in a way that helps them address the issues that crop up. If something's not working, you fall back on that experimental mindset and try something else. You improvise and listen to how the audience reacts—and you keep at it.

Listen for What Matters Most

We've all attended meetings where the person in charge goes in with a list of topics to cover and plows through the checklist. This is the small *a* agenda. But what if a coworker in the meeting has just learned of a family death and is visibly distressed during the meeting? Everyone else is likely aware of the big *A* Agenda, which is to show compassion for the colleague who is hurting.

Leaders must always step back and be mindful of the scene in front of them. What's truly important here? When I coach clients, I often say, "Imagine it's thirty years from now. What will truly matter when you look back on this moment?" In virtually every circumstance, this helps the client separate the agenda from the Agenda to identify what truly matters—and matters most.

In the end, inspired leaders—be they Composer, Conductor, Performer, Producer, or Fan—give everything to their role, and they listen and respond to feedback while doing so. They are receptive to what's expressed by their fellow Ensemble members. They enter into Maestro Mode, where those little *a* agendas give way to the big *A* ones.

Part of what's exciting about a live-music performance is that no one ever knows exactly what will happen. In the early 1980s, U2 was still a relatively unknown act and the lead singer, Bono, as the *Los Angeles Times* would later recount, "went to dangerous extremes to forge a bond with the audience." On YouTube, there's an interview with Bono, recorded after he performed at the US Festival in 1983 (organized by Apple cofounder Steve Wozniak). In the interview, Bono is asked about a moment during "Sunday Bloody Sunday" when he climbed the side of the stage and waved a white flag from a hundred feet up. Here's what he had to say:

> Management and the rest of the band told me it was a stupid thing to do, that the rest of the tour was at risk. But I felt in a festival where there's 200,000 people watching you, basically only about half that, maybe three quarters of that, are feeling what you're doing musically. And I felt that if we could walk, could take a white flag, which is everything we stand for… to the highest point in the US Festival, well, I think I felt that even the people who were buying that hotdog, even the people who were asleep, would look up. And they did. In the entire crowd, that moment was unified. That white flag, as I placed it on the top, and I threw it over into the crowd and they caught it. I felt that that was an important thing to do. I mean, I threw the song away. The song just became the soundtrack to that movement, but I felt it was worth it, and I think the crowd would agree.

The big *A*, in terms of its paramount importance, also stands for Audience. And if the audience feels something and reacts in a positive way, you've done your job. When that happens, bravo. Enjoy the moment. Accept the cheers. Then get ready for an encore and the next performance.

CODA

AS I WROTE at the start of this book, the question I hear more than any other is "Why music?" Why is it a good way to teach people about leadership? Now that you've read this book, I hope I've convinced you how music maps well onto the leadership behaviors with which you're already familiar. In my experience, music has proven to be an effective way to get people to think differently about leadership. To illustrate this, let me tell you a story in which this approach proved highly impactful for an organization. After that, I invite you to experiment and put these principles into practice in your organization.

It was the late spring of 2022, and a good friend and colleague sent me an urgent email with the subject "Help! Music + Leadership needed." We quickly arranged for a time to meet, and he explained to me that his organization, after nearly three years of working almost 100 percent remotely due to the Covid pandemic, wanted to hold an in-person strategic planning session off-site on the theme of "Shared Success." But they wanted something different for this event, something unique and engaging. They wanted an experience that would enable the participants to learn about themselves and each other so they could co-create a shared vision of success that would leave everyone inspired about how to lead with impact.

As I listened carefully (using the techniques I've explored in this book), I also learned from my friend that after working through the challenges of Covid, his employees were feeling exhausted and disconnected from their teams and needed to be reengaged and motivated with a renewed mission, vision, and set of values. He said, "I'm intrigued by how you use music as a lens for leadership, but how will this all work? Oh, and by the way, this is scheduled for three weeks from now. And did I happen to mention this event will be held in Georgia"—a different state than my home of Illinois—"and there will be over two hundred people in attendance?"

Our team at Audira quickly went to work integrating the concepts we've discussed throughout this book. The big day arrived, and soon after the audience members took their seats, the lights dimmed, the curtain dropped, and the Audira band performed an original song that infused melody, harmony, volume, tempo, and lyrics in keeping with the theme of the workshop.

> You have your whole life and your dreams in front of you
> I can't wait to see what your anthem turns into
> Your tone and tempo will reveal themselves to you
> I can't wait to see what your anthem turns into

For those in the audience who were expecting a dull kickoff to another boring off-site event, they were happily surprised and curious. The audience was primed and pumped!

After playing with the band, I put down my guitar and provided a brief and interactive discussion with the audience on the power of listening (using musical examples) and the Ensemble Model. As I explored the concepts with the audience, I invited them to share personal stories in which they could draw parallels between music and leadership. And there was no shortage of contribution to that discussion. One participant said they were looking forward to practicing harmonization (connection) with other leaders in the organization. Another leader mentioned being curious to work with their department and experiment with expanding their leadership dynamic range. Quite a few other good examples from participants followed.

The audience was then divided into ensembles (groups of eight to ten individuals), given musical instruments, and, with the help of facilitators (expert musicians), asked to compose, conduct, produce, and perform their own Leadership Anthems for fellow audience members (fans). No musical experience was required, by the way, as the amazing musician-facilitators helped guide participants throughout the process.

These anthems could be any type of song, as long as they integrated lyrics and music that somehow spoke to their organization's values, mission, and vision. A simple example of a Leadership Anthem in everyday life might be a fun, engaging statement that encapsulates a team's mission, vision, and values. Here's an example of a Leadership Anthem from a team who felt passionately about inclusivity and belonging:

> Giving everybody a voice
> Encourages the river to grow
> Having compassion for each other
> Inspires the ebb and flow

> Every journey involves failure and detours
> Sometimes that just what we need
> Stepping up and stepping back
> It helps when we let others lead
>
> Giving everybody a voice
> Encourages the river to grow
> Having compassion for each other
> Inspires the ebb and flow

During this portion of the event, participants played instruments (applying active listening, along with experimentation), wrote lyrics (composing a shared vision), organized different roles (conducted), coached one another (served as producers), and finally performed for their fans. As each ensemble performed, their fans leapt to their feet and cheered.

After all of the ensembles performed, we asked each group to reflect on how they would carry forward and sustain their Leadership Anthem. In response, they described creating accountability duos, trios, and quartets that would help them maintain the momentum.

Following the event, we solicited feedback from participants in conjunction with the client's team. The responses were overwhelmingly positive—they were real fans, to put it mildly. Aside from identifying the experience as having been unique, participants expressed how they walked away inspired, reconnected, and excited to amplify the impact of our work together going forward.

I started this journey of seeing leadership through the lens of music as a way to assess my own situation and goals. This lens enabled me to envision, think more deeply about, and work towards the impact I want to make in the world. When

I recognized and appreciated how well it worked, I saw that it would work for others too.

My wife, Michelle, and I had a hypothesis, which was that musicians would intuitively understand this framework but non-musicians might not get it, at least initially. But I've learned, through listening, that our hypothesis was wrong. Musicians do love this framework, but non-musicians seem to love it, too—and learn the most from it.

I learn from practice and from the people with whom I work. To that end, I want to hear about how the concepts we've explored together, including the Ensemble Model, work for you. Send me an email. Let me know what happens when you put these ideas into practice. I always love hearing from people who adopt the musical mindset, and I want to hear just as much about what doesn't work as what does.

As John Lennon sang, imagine what the world could be like. To any left-brain skeptics who might say that's naive, I would encourage you to think about game theory and through the possibilities. Organizationally speaking, let's say that a company isn't listening to its employees while it extracts as much energy from them as possible in the name of productivity. Where will that lead? Those employees will feel less engaged and leave. Productivity will fall, and competitors will pick up that talent.

But this doesn't have to be the case if you instead imagine a different future. The Wright brothers worked on bicycles while they dreamed about balancing on flying machines. Gandhi and Martin Luther King Jr. refused to accept that their goals could only be achieved through violence. This book ultimately isn't about music: it's about the mindset behind it. That's what I want you to rehearse now. Listen. Write your song. Find your bandmates. Practice, practice, practice. And don't be afraid to improvise. After all, why not?

ACKNOWLEDGMENTS

YOU ROCK! This composition would not have been possible without the love, support, and encouragement of so many amazing souls I've had the honor of meeting along this journey called life. In keeping with the spirit of this book, I'd like to express deep gratitude to everyone in the following ensembles.

My Family Ensemble

First and foremost, I am grateful to my parents, John M. Kohler Jr. and Lucile "Snooky" Kohler, for their enduring support that ultimately made this endeavor possible. Dad's lived values and discipline, along with Mom's curiosity and creativity, were instrumental in shaping who I am today and in the creation of this book. To my brothers, Jeff, Matt, and Andrew, I can't thank you enough for your mentorship throughout life and your enduring championing through each chapter. I would be remiss if I didn't thank my grandparents (Grandmommy, Papa John, Nana, Grandpa Jake) for their artistic and intellectual impact that contributed to this effort. And to Lilly, I am grateful for your enduring wisdom, grace, and partnership in life's high and low notes.

To my duet partner for life, Shelly, I am eternally grateful for the inspiration, collaboration, and shaping of this work. Audira and this book would not have been what it is without your incredible melodies and harmonies along the way. To my greatest compositions, Jonah and Lucas, thank you for inspiring and teaching me something new every day. I hope this book reflects a bit of what I've learned from you. To Dixie, Peaches, Meghan, Ozzy, Mocha, and Kodi, a big woof to you all! And to my entire extended family, thank you for your enduring fandom along the way.

My Music Ensemble

To the countless incredible composers, conductors, performers, and producers I've had the honor of playing and co-creating with, this book was truly inspired by our many jams. To ABBA, Edward Van Halen, Ozzy Osbourne, and the numerous artists that have inspired me along the way, thank you for starting it all for me! Also, in semichronological order, to my bandmates: Charles, Brett, Will, Robbie, Mike, Aaron, Everett, Ameet, Steve, Andy, Pete, Brian, Kevin, Pat, Gino & crew, Jeremy & the Midnight Thieves, and all those whom I've failed to include due to old-age memory lapse.

A huge shout out to Liam Davis, my incredibly gifted friend, co-creator, and producer, for helping me make my musical dreams a reality and for introducing me to so many insanely talented musicians so that I could bring my music to life, all of which helped inspire many of the ideas in this book.

My Leadership Ensemble

I have been so fortunate to have had some incredible Jedi leadership guides along the way. In no particular order, I am grateful to my friends and mentors at Shure Incorporated,

Digital Innovations, Weber-Stephen Products, Bridge Partnership (Michael), Keystone Partners (Nancy), and the incredible coaching and team development clients I've supported over the years.

A huge thank-you to the University of Chicago Booth School of Business for teaching me so much and for the opportunity to jam together. I am eternally grateful to Professor Harry Davis for his deep wisdom, joy, and shared passion for music and experimentation, along with his entire Leadership Studio team (Nancy, Ed, Becki, Chelsea). A big rock-on to my friends at the Davis Center (Carolyn) and Polsky Center (Gorana) for your kind invitation to improvise together like the jazz greats.

Of course, to Co-Active Training Institute (my incredible coach supervisors) and Starlings, thank you for helping me look within, grow, and make a small impact in the world.

And to Don Vanpool for sharing the journey of supporting others together.

My Writing Ensemble

To just a few of my favorite writers who ignited my literary flame: Camus, Sartre, Stephen King, Mark Manson, David Brooks, Rick Rubin, Ryan Holiday, and so many more I don't have the space to list here—thank you for continuously quenching my thirst for possibility.

And for this book itself: huge thanks to Shelly, for your early brainstorming and endless marketing support; to Lou Carlozo, your unmatched "composition and production" skills, including content-shaping, research, and storytelling, are incredible; to Emily, Sarah, and Rachel, your unique gifts of editing my musings into something coherent brought this book to an entirely new level. To my additional co-creators at Page Two: Jesse, Beate, Meghan, Tessa, Viktoria, Jennifer, Madelaine, Jay, Natassja, and the entire team, thank you for helping simplify the complex world of publishing and for bringing this book to life. I've learned so much from all of you!

The Audira Ensemble

To Shelly, Michelle, and Kim, everything in this book is thanks to you and what we discovered together. To our advisory board: Melanie Hill, Brian and Debbie Hall, Howard Brandeisky, Ameet Mallik, Rosa Greenwood, Rob Anstey, Liam Davis, and all of our facilitators and musicians, thank you for your guidance, superpowers, and passion. To our greatest interns and future leaders, Jonah and Lucas, thank you for inspiring us in terms of what the future of leadership looks like.

The Clients and Fans Ensemble

To the numerous leaders, clients, teams, and organizations I've had the honor of supporting, please know that I've learned so much from each of you. To those who read this book, I am grateful and would love to hear your harmonies. Feel free to send me your thoughts at info@audiralabs.com.

Rock on!

NOTES

Overture

p. 5   *Music has been around since*: Kimberley Sena Moore, "Which Came First: Music or Language?" *Psychology Today*, September 20, 2012, https://www.psychologytoday.com/ca/blog/your-musical-self/201209/which-came-first-music-or-language.

Chapter 1: Feel the Music

p. 24   *That led to a Great Resignation*: Aaron De Smet, Bonnie Dowling, Bryan Hancock, and Bill Schaninger, "The Great Attrition Is Making Hiring Harder. Are You Searching the Right Talent Pools?" *McKinsey Quarterly*, July 13, 2022, https://www.mckinsey.com/capabilities/people-and-organizational-performance/our-insights/the-great-attrition-is-making-hiring-harder-are-you-searching-the-right-talent-pools.

p. 25   *According to Gostick and Elton's survey*: Kellie Wong, "12 Best Practices for Peer-to-Peer Recognition," Achievers, August 12, 2023, https://www.achievers.com/blog/peer-to-peer-recognition/.

Chapter 2: Ear Training

p. 28   *In* Harvard Business Review, *Professor*: Robin Abrahams and Boris Groysberg, "How to Become a Better Listener," *Harvard Business Review*, December 21, 2021, https://hbr.org/2021/12/how-to-become-a-better-listener.

p. 28 *In McKinsey Quarterly, the now-former dean*: Bernard T. Ferrari, "The Executive's Guide to Better Listening," *McKinsey Quarterly*, February 1, 2012, https://www.mckinsey.com/featured-insights/leadership/the-executives-guide-to-better-listening.

p. 28 *In* Forbes, *coach Rachel Wells presented*: Rachel Wells, "Active Listening Skills: What They Are and Why They're Important," *Forbes*, September 4, 2023, https://www.forbes.com/sites/rachelwells/2023/09/04/active-listening-skills-what-they-are-and-why-theyre-important/?sh=5a04580666d1.

p. 28 *"Good listeners are like trampolines*: Jack Zenger and Joseph Folkman, "What Great Listeners Actually Do," *Harvard Business Review*, July 14, 2016, https://hbr.org/2016/07/what-great-listeners-actually-do.

p. 29 *As legendary violinist and performer*: "Biography," Itzhak Perlman, https://itzhakperlman.com/biography/.

p. 33 *"Most people do not listen with*: Stephen Covey, *The 7 Habits of Highly Effective People* (Simon & Schuster, 2004), 239.

p. 35 *In 2013, three Florida State professors*: Cary Stothart, Ainsley Mitchum, and Courtney Yehnert, "The Attentional Cost of Receiving a Cell Phone Notification," *Journal of Experimental Psychology: Human Perception and Performance* 41, no. 4 (2015), 893–897, https://doi.org/10.1037/xhp0000100.

p. 35 *half of the undergraduate students interviewed*: Elena Neiterman and Christine Zaza, "A Mixed Blessing? Students' and Instructors' Perspectives about Off-Task Technology Use in the Academic Classroom," *The Canadian Journal for the Scholarship of Teaching and Learning* 10, no. 1 (2019), https://doi.org/10.5206/cjsotl-rcacea.2019.1.8002.

p. 38 *Put simply, strong listeners avoid*: For a fascinating deep-dive on this topic, check out psychologist and economist Daniel Kahneman's classic *Thinking, Fast and Slow*.

p. 38 *call cognitive biases*: "Cognitive Biases," The Decision Lab, https://thedecisionlab.com/biases.

p. 39 *Actual data showed that travelers*: Aric Jenkins, "Which Is Safer: Airplanes or Cars?," *Fortune*, July 20, 2017, https://fortune.com/2017/07/20/are-airplanes-safer-than-cars/.

p. 41   *a form that has its roots in*: MasterClass, "What Is Call and Response in Music?" August 26, 2021, https://www.masterclass.com/articles/what-is-call-and-response-in-music#735EQTvyb7gdcaxIusdYrH.

p. 44   *"The second rule of improvisation*: Tina Fey, *Bossypants* (Little, Brown & Company, 2011), 84.

p. 46   *Groundbreaking research in the 1960s*: "Mehrabian's 7-38-55 Communication Model," *The World of Work Podcast*, episode 22, 42:10, https://worldofwork.io/2019/07/mehrabians-7-38-55-communication-model.

p. 47   *not even the* New York Times *reporter*: Michael Pollak, "The Origins of That Famous Carnegie Hall Joke," *The New York Times*, November 27, 2009, https://www.nytimes.com/2009/11/29/nyregion/29fyi.html.

Chapter 3: The Audira Ensemble Model

p. 50   *named the Audira Ensemble Model*: This name was inspired by my dear mentor and friend Professor Harry Davis at the University of Chicago Booth School of Business, where I had the opportunity to co-create with him in his Leadership Studio class.

Chapter 4: The Composer

p. 58   *One of her biggest hits, "I Will*: "Dolly Parton Is Burning Up, Not Burning Out (Transcript)," from *WorkLife* with Adam Grant, TED online, April 5, 2022, https://www.ted.com/podcasts/worklife/dolly-parton-is-burning-up-not-burning-out-transcript.

p. 59   *"a leader is both a singer and*: Jim Crupi, "What Great Leadership and Music Have in Common," Ideas .TED.com, October 18, 2016, https://ideas.ted.com/what-great-leadership-and-music-have-in-common.

Chapter 5: The Conductor

p. 73 *Between August 2020 and February 2021*: Anjel Vahratian, Stephen J. Blumberg, Emily P. Terlizzi, and Jeannine S. Schiller, "Symptoms of Anxiety or Depressive Disorder and Use of Mental Health Care Among Adults During the COVID-19 Pandemic—United States, August 2020–February 2021," *Morbidity and Mortality Weekly Report* (CDC) 70, no. 13 (April 2, 2021), 490–494, https://www.cdc.gov/mmwr/volumes/70/wr/mm7013e2.htm.

p. 76 *"Make no little plans; they have*: "The Development of Cities of the Future," an address to the Town Planning Conference in London, October 1910, as quoted in "Stirred by Burnham, Democracy Champion," *The Chicago Record-Herald*, October 15, 1910.

p. 83 *"From now on, [choosing my*: Quoted from a 1991 speech in Lisa Girion, "GE Succession a Leadership Lesson," *Los Angeles Times*, December 3, 2000, https://www.latimes.com/archives/la-xpm-2000-dec-03-wp-60548-story.html.

Chapter 6: The Performer

p. 87 *"The music is not in the notes*: This quote has also been attributed to Claude Debussy; whichever great composer said it, the wisdom in it is sound!

p. 91 *In his must-read book*: Marshall Goldsmith with Mark Reiter, *What Got You Here Won't Get You There: How Successful People Become Even More Successful* (New York: Hyperion, 2007).

p. 93 *"What does it take to play music*: Robert Rowat and Holly Gordon, "Remembering Jerry Granelli, the Legendary Drummer behind *A Charlie Brown Christmas*," CBC Music, July 21, 2021, https://www.cbc.ca/music/remembering-jerry-granelli-the-legendary-drummer-behind-a-charlie-brown-christmas-1.6110882.

Chapter 7: The Producer

p. 103 *"Rick Rubin is one of the*: *60 Minutes*, "In Shangri-La with Music Producer Rick Rubin," interview with Anderson Cooper, aired May 28, 2023, on CBS News, https://www.cbsnews.com/news/rick-rubin-60-minutes-transcript-2023-05-28/.

p. 104   *"I don't even know what a*: J. Freedom du Lac, "The 'Song Doctor' Is In," *The Washington Post*, January 14, 2006, https://www.washingtonpost.com/archive/lifestyle/style/2006/01/15/the-song-doctor-is-in-span-classbankheadfrom-audioslave-to-neil-diamond-recording-artists-know-producer-rick-rubins-touch-is-a-powerful-tonicspan/424fd5ef-2b05-4240-8564-6e6cdb284bf4/.

Chapter 8: The Fan

p. 114   *"For the longest time, we*: Pat Smear, "Interview with Dave Grohl," *Guitar World*, August 1997, reproduced online by Alan di Perna, September 2, 2022, https://www.guitarworld.com/features/dave-grohl-kurt-cobain-pat-smear-1997.

p. 115   *At a 1969 press conference*: Michael McDonough, "Why Is Elvis Called "the King of Rock 'n' Roll"?" *Britannica* online, https://www.britannica.com/story/why-is-elvis-called-the-king-of-rock-n-roll.

p. 115   *"Led Zeppelin is the greatest*: As quoted in Scott Cohen, "Queen's Freddie Mercury Shopping for an Image in London," *Circus Magazine*, April 1975.

p. 115   *"I was asking myself, 'Do I*: Rob Duguay, "The Dig Interview: Cory Wong," *DigBoston*, February 24, 2023, https://digboston.com/the-dig-interview-cory-wong/.

p. 116   *the photo was posted online under*: "Dave Grohl Goes to Metallica Concert like an Ordinary Dude," *Vintage Heavy Metal*, https://www.vintageheavymetal.com/article/dave-grohl-metallica-concert/.

p. 120   *Starkey and his friends made*: Mark Bennett, "B-Sides: Birth of an Army: A Revolution Had Humble Beginnings 30 Years Ago in a Terre Haute Basement," *Tribune-Star*, November 17, 2005, https://www.tribstar.com/news/news_columns/b-sides-birth-of-an-army-a-revolution-had-humble-beginnings-30-years-ago-in/article_ddd71095-609e-5be9-ad9d-938225d3781b.html.

p. 120   *Amid all the attention, Kiss*: "We Salute Kiss Army Co-founder & Commander in Chief Bill Starkey," *I'm Music Magazine*, November 29, 2023, https://im-musicmagazine.com/f/we-salute-kiss-army-co-founder-commander-inchief-bill-starkey?blogcatego=.

p. 121 *After thirty-plus years, increasing deafness meant*: Matt Everitt, "Interview with Brian Johnson," *The First Time*, BBC Radio 6, November 27, 2022, as discussed in "AC/DC's Brian Johnson Details Technology Which Helped Him Overcome His Hearing Loss," BlabberMouth.net, November 28, 2022, https://blabbermouth.net/news/ac-dcs-brian-johnson-details-technology-which-helped-him-overcome-his-hearing-loss.

Chapter 9: The Tour

p. 124 *"Work is love made visible*: Kahlil Gibran, "The Prophet (1923)," Poets.org, https://poets.org/poem/work-4.

p. 125 *The late Steven Schnall, the*: Matthew De Paula, "Progress, Not Perfection: How a Twentysomething Marketing Entrepreneur Helped Transform a Small Community Development Financial Institution into a Nimble Digital Innovator," *American Banker*, June 2020, https://arizent.brightspotcdn.com/4f/17/65a70be34f35aebd81a070331c72/abm-0620.pdf.

p. 126 *He holds that this "deep practice"*: Daniel Coyle, "An Excerpt from *The Talent Code*—Chapter 1: The Sweet Spot," https://danielcoyle.com/excerpt-talent-code/.

p. 129 *In the early 1980s, U2 was*: Robert Hilburn, "U2's Perilous Life at the Top," *Los Angeles Times*, March 17, 1985, https://www.latimes.com/archives/la-xpm-1985-03-17-ca-35281-story.html.

p. 130 *Management and the rest of the band told me*: Historic Films Stock Footage Archive, "Bono Interview at US Festival 1983 U2," YouTube video, 8:42, September 23, 2013, https://www.youtube.com/watch?v=ZAg-AZDTxqA.

SOURCES AND RESOURCES

Playlist

To help inspire your leadership journey, I've created a playlist of a few of my musical favorites. Check it out and crank it up! spoti.fi/3znwcHZ

Books

This Is Your Brain on Music: The Science of a Human Obsession by Daniel Levitin

A Leadership Canvas by Professor Harry Davis

The Four Agreements: A Practical Guide to Personal Freedom by Don Miguel Ruiz

What Got You Here Won't Get You There: How Successful People Become Even More Successful! by Marshall Goldsmith with Mark Reiter

The Music Lesson: A Spiritual Search for Growth through Music by Victor L. Wooten

The Creative Act: A Way of Being by Rick Rubin

The Daily Stoic: 366 Meditations on Wisdom, Perseverance, and the Art of Living by Ryan Holiday

*The Subtle Art of Not Giving a F*ck: A Counterintuitive Approach to Living a Good Life* by Mark Manson

The Second Mountain: The Quest for a Moral Life by David Brooks

Leadership from the Inside Out: Becoming a Leader for Life by Kevin Cashman

Man's Search for Meaning by Viktor E. Frankl

Thinking, Fast and Slow by Daniel Kahneman

Tribes: We Need You to Lead Us by Seth Godin

Atomic Habits: An Easy & Proven Way to Build Good Habits & Break Bad Ones by James Clear

Team of Rivals: The Political Genius of Abraham Lincoln by Doris Kearns Goodwin

The First 90 Days: Proven Strategies for Getting Up to Speed Faster and Smarter by Michael D. Watkins

Steve Jobs by Walter Isaacson

Podcasts

Coaching for Leaders, hosted by Dave Stachowiak

Broken Record, hosted by Justin Richman with interviews by Rick Rubin, Malcolm Gladwell, and Bruce Headlam

The Art of Happiness with Arthur Brooks

Videos

Benjamin Zander: The Transformative Power of Classical Music, TED Talk

Stephen Kohler: Knowledge Speaks while Wisdom Listens, TEDx Talk

Newsletter

The Marginalian by Maria Popova

Leadership Development Assessments

The Myers Briggs (MBTI) Assessment (https://www.themyersbriggs.com)

Hogan Assessments (https://www.hoganassessments.com/)

Gallup's CliftonStrengths assessment (https://www.gallup.com/cliftonstrengths/en/254033/strengthsfinder.aspx)

PHOTO: JENNY MAY STRINGER

ABOUT THE AUTHOR

STEPHEN KOHLER loves mixing both left- and right-brain pursuits. His background includes such left-brain hits as earning his MBA from the University of Chicago Booth School of Business, serving as a global leader at Fortune 100, midsize, and startup organizations, and becoming a certified executive leadership coach. From the right brain, he brings his unique perspective as a musician, songwriter, and performer, along with an undergraduate degree in philosophy from Northwestern University. He has combined these analytical and creative sides as the founder and CEO of Audira Labs (audiralabs.com), a firm he started to explore how music can serve as a method for inspiring corporate leaders to deliver their best leadership performances—one value, collaboration, common purpose, and listening skill at a time. Stephen has taken this show on the road as a two-time TEDx speaker, a guest lecturer at the University of Chicago's Booth Leadership Studio, and a keynote speaker for corporate events. His music is available on Spotify and other streaming platforms.

Don't Stop the Music

Do you want to take the next step towards being a leader who leads with impact?

Please join us—both on tour and backstage. Connect with Audira, the company I founded, and me across the universe for more: **audiralabs.com**

You may also follow me here: **stephenjkohler.com**

Follow Audira Labs and me:
in Audira Labs (linkedin.com/company/audiralabs/)
in Stephen Kohler (linkedin.com/in/kohlerstephen/)
f Audira Labs (facebook.com/audiralabs)

Join our book community newsletter:
audiralabs.com/book-community/

Invite me to join YOUR band
How can I support you? Whether by speaking engagements, workshops, or one-to-one executive coaching—I am ready for all of it, and each experience is specially crafted for you. Hot tip: we have a smoking band we bring for events. Learn more at audiralabs.com.

Contact me
Yes, I check my own email. Send me a note!
skohler@audiralabs.com

Check out my music
I don't just *talk* about music. I am also a recording artist and performer. Find me on all of the streaming platforms, socials, and at stephenkohlermusic.com.
▶ ◎ ● ● ♪ ♫Music

www.ingramcontent.com/pod-product-compliance
Lightning Source LLC
Chambersburg PA
CBHW060609080526
44585CB00013B/745